THE NEW
RED
LEGIONS

Recent Titles in
Contributions in Political Science
Series Editor: Bernard K. Johnpoll

THE NEW
RED
LEGIONS A Survey Data
_____ Source Book

RICHARD A. GABRIEL

CONTRIBUTIONS IN POLITICAL SCIENCE, NUMBER 44

GREENWOOD PRESS

WESTPORT, CONNECTICUT ● LONDON, ENGLAND

Library of Congress Cataloging in Publication Data

Gabriel, Richard A.
    The new Red legions: A survey data source book.

(Contributions in political science; no. 44
ISSN 0147-1066)
    Bibliography: p.
    Includes index.
    1. Russia (1923-   U.S.S.R.). Armiia. 2. Soldiers
—Russia. 3. Russians in foreign countries. 1. Title
II. Series.
UA772.G22   355'.00947   79-24458
ISBN 0-313-21497-2 lib. bdg.

Library of Congress Catalog Card Number: 79-24458
ISBN: 0-313-21497-2
ISSN: 0147-1066

First published in 1980

Greenwood Press
A division of Congressional Information Service, Inc.
88 Post Road West, Westport, Connecticut 06881

Printed in the United States of America

10 9 8 7 6 5 4 3 2 1

To My Beloved Katherine
Whom I Love Beyond All Measure

Contents

Foreword _____

In this century the Russian Army has collapsed seriously on two occasions: In the context of the World War I debacle, historians have generally pointed to the ineptitude of Tsarist leadership. In the second instance, the collapse of the Soviet Army against German forces in World War II, the collapse has been broadly attributed to Stalin's leadership failures. Though it is recognized that in each case a different combination of factors played a role in the military destruction of Soviet forces—and the debate continues as to what factors were most significant—there can be no question that in both instances masses of Russian soldiers were slaughtered, thousands captured, and large amounts of Russian war material destroyed.

Making use of both overt and covert sources, modern intelligence estimates of Soviet military capabilities are usually accomplished by quantifying the number of divisions, types of soldiers, and quality of military equipment available to the enemy. Despite the effectiveness of this procedure there exists no disciplined approach to determine what actually makes the modern Soviet Army tick. There is no method for examining the social relationships among members of the Soviet Army, their attitudes toward military life, or the degree to which they possess the psychological characteristic of unit cohesion. Accordingly, until now it has been impossible to assess with any accuracy the extent to which Soviet units can be expected to remain cohesive in battle.

Professor Gabriel's book *The New Red Legions: A Survey Data Source Book*, goes a long way in solving the problem. Though the author admits that much remains to be done and that the data have limits, he manages, for the first time anywhere in the West, to employ empirical data to treat this elusive but crucially important aspect of the Soviet military force. The uniqueness of this book is furthered by the author's recognized expertise as a leading analyst on the subject of military organizations, their leadership, and their combat effectiveness. This analytical expertise—combined with his collection and evaluation of data that is normally masked by Soviet counterintelligence efforts—produces a unique view of the Soviet Army seen through the eyes of its own soldiers. All this makes this latest book by Professor Gabriel very special and a major contribution to our knowledge of the Soviet Army.

This book is full of surprises even for those who are familiar with the literature on the Soviet Army. *The New Red Legions* assaults much of the conventional wisdom about the Soviet military and can be expected to stir heated controversy among experts both inside and outside the intelligence community. For those unfamiliar with the subject it will surely be an excursion into a brutal, insensitive world where the military ethos is still locked in the eighteenth and nineteenth centuries.

No one, not even intelligence analysts, can ever be absolutely sure what really goes on inside the Soviet Army. Yet, this book offers some rare documented glimpses into one of the most hidden and mysterious of Soviet social institutions, glimpses that have heretofore escaped analysis. The startling suggestion of this study is that the Soviet Army may have grave systemic weaknesses that can be exploited by Western forces on the future battlefield. Should this book's conclusions remain intact as more data are developed, it will become a classic in the field of literature on the Soviet military.

For the moment, however, despite the fact that the Soviet Army projects itself as the best-equipped, largest tactical and strategic military force in the world, Dr. Gabriel has reminded us that the Soviet soldier is by no means a "man of steel." Thanks to this pioneering effort, Western analysts can now legitimately speculate whether the man of steel has entrails of straw and whether there are unseen fissures in the Soviet Army that would compel it to collapse under pressure—for the third time in this century.

Robert E. Bartos
Chief, Intelligence Division
Office of the Assistant Chief of Staff for Intelligence
United States Army

Acknowledgments __

Many people stand behind a work of this type. There is Morris Janowitz of the University of Chicago, who has always encouraged me in my work. Sam Sarkesian, my friend and colleague, has been central to this effort, for it was he who encouraged the Inter-University Seminar on Armed Forces and Society to lend financial support to this study. Nothing could have been done without the aid of Ken Gabel and the Jewish Community Center of Manchester, New Hampshire, who arranged access to other émigré service agencies here and abroad. Slava Lerner, a neophyte scholar, provided invaluable assistance in interpreting many of the letters and comments received from Russian respondents. A number of institutions helped greatly by providing resources of other sorts. In this regard special thanks are owed the Harvard Russian Research Center for first recognizing the merit of the work and providing a platform from which I could express my ideas. The United States Army War College, the Army Command and General Staff School, the Canadian Forces Staff College, and the Royal Military Academy at Sandhurst all contributed by allowing me to offer my ideas in their forums and to take advantage of the responses of their students. Thanks are owed to *Military Review* and *Parameters*, which published my initial research—the reaction to which fired my enthusiasm for a wider study. I am most grateful to John Keegan, Chris Donnelley, Senator Sam Nunn, Jeff Record, Congressman Robin Beard, Colonel Robert Bartos, and Chris Jones for having read the manuscript and offering their comments. I am appreciative of St. Anselm's College for providing a tranquil and unhurried environment in which to write. Paul Savage, my friend, and John D'Espinosa, who helped me repair my porch, also made significant contributions in their own right as did Shannon Larson, my research assistant, who typed much of the manuscript. Finally, my sincere thanks are offered to my brother officers in the U.S. Army intelligence services who helped me when help was needed. They deserve the respect they have in the mouths of the chosen few.

Richard A. Gabriel
Manchester, New Hampshire
1980

Studying
the
Soviet
Army

It is not often that researchers get the opportunity to make their source material available to other interested scholars. Fortunately, the opportunity to publish *The New Red Legions: A Survey Data Source Book* provides an opportunity to make the first systematic, empirical, longitudinal, survey-research study dealing with the attitudes of Soviet soldiers available to the ranks of interested historians, military sociologists, and defense analysts. Contained within these pages are not only the statistical results of that two-year study, but the means by which the serious researcher can extract the original data files and transfer them to his or her own computer banks so that further analysis of the data can be undertaken. In this sense the work bears a strong resemblance to what Banks and Textor tried to do when they published their *Cross-Polity Survey*.

This *Source Book* is the direct result of the publication of the work, *The New Red Legions: An Attitudinal Portrait of the Soviet Soldier*. That earlier work contains an analysis of the survey data and, hopefully, will become a baseline against which further analysis of the data can be compared. Being right in one's assessments in not nearly as important as stimulating—even through one's own errors—further assessments generated by other more competent scholars.

I undertook this work essentially because it seemed that much of the past work dealing with the "mind of the Soviet soldier" was lacking in empirical precision. What was needed was a different kind of study, one that would use past efforts as its point of departure and would proceed more empirically toward the gathering of key elements of information dealing with a range of socio-psychological factors largely absent in most treatments of the Soviet Army.

This *Source Book* represents the first successful study in which large numbers of Soviet soldiers were interviewed in a systematic attempt to obtain a new perspective on the Soviet Army as seen from within through the eyes of the Soviet soldier. It is the first attempt to "get inside the Soviet soldier's head" and it is the first study in which a researcher has been able to arrange a body of empirical data dealing with the subject longitudinally. Thus a range of socio-psychological elements of comparison—the attitude structure of the Soviet soldier, his feelings, his thoughts, his evaluations of the Soviet Army, and his experiences within that army—can be compared along several dimensions across a forty-year period. By using the survey approach to obtain sufficient numbers of indepth, questionnaire interviews with Soviet soldiers, this study can go further than previous studies and evaluate the Soviet Army and the Soviet military experience as the Soviet soldier saw it and experienced it. Respondents in the sample cover a range of military service beginning prior to World War II and extending through 1978. Perhaps most importantly, the use of survey research techniques allowed the researcher to gather information about intangible elements of the Soviet military experience which have so often been overlooked or minimized in past studies. For the first time this study allows the construction of an accurate attitudinal portrait of the Soviet soldier's regard for his military life.

Events conspired to aid greatly in the successful completion of this work. In the past the flow of émigrés from the Soviet Union was merely a trickle and tended to consist largely of military defectors who were able to gain access to a Western border. In 1971-1972, when the Soviet Union adopted a more relaxed attitude toward Jewish emigration, the number of émigrés increased dramatically and has become significant since then. Approximately thirty thousand émigrés a year exit Russia for destinations in Israel, Italy, Canada, and the United States. These people provide the social scientist with an excellent opportunity to examine the Soviet Army through the experiences of its former members using empirical survey research techniques.

The argument for using this approach is basic. In the Soviet Union military service is required of all citizens. From what we know of the actual operation of the conscription system, all but approximately 12 percent of conscript age males between eighteen and twenty-four actually serve in the military. It seems reasonable that the émigrés would also have served in the Soviet military. Since the émigré population contains all age groups, ranging from young children to men over eighty, one would expect that a sample of émigrés would have performed their military service at vastly different periods of time. Accordingly, some would have served in the pre-World War II Russian Army, some would have served during World War II, some would have served in the post-Stalin era, some would have served during the Hungarian revolt, some would have served during the Cuban missile crisis and the Czech invasion, and some would have served as recently as 1978. Further, if the Soviet conscript system is working as designed then a sample of émigrés should have served in all branches of the military. Also, they should be statistically distributed as to the number of officers, non-commissioned officers, and enlisted men. Moreover, the data should stratify on the educational variable with some being college graduates, some being high school graduates, some being technical school graduates, and some finishing only secondary school. A reasonable number should have been commanders and occupied supervisory positions, and a reasonable number should have had combat experience while a reasonable number should not. In short, if the Soviet conscript system is working correctly then a sample of those who have left the Soviet Union over the last seven years should reflect as full a range of military experiences as any other Soviet soldiers or as any other group in the Soviet Union. Therefore, the opportunity to obtain their views and experiences through a systematic survey should produce a data file whose contents are accurately representative of the military experiences of the average soldier.

The actual sample selection process was direct and simple—or so it seemed initially. The first task was to open communications with sixty-four émigré service agencies in the United States, Italy, and Canada to petition their help in obtaining the names and addresses of recently arrived respondents. A "recently arrived respondent" is defined here as anyone who had arrived in the United States during the last five years. The goal was to obtain an accurate and current list of possible respondents in order to contact them directly or through a mailed questionnaire. These efforts resulted in an agreement with most of these agencies to undertake one of two tasks: either provide a direct mailing list so that it could be used to contact respondents directly or agree to distribute questionnaires to respondents living within the agency's area of responsibility. This second option was a concession to the concern for confidentiality among émigré agencies. Utilizing both methods, a total of 1,059 questionnaires was issued. The period of distribution and return of questionnaires was set at three months. As events proceeded, about 400 direct mail questionnaires were sent while the remaining 659 were distributed by the local service agencies.

At the end of the three-month period returns showed a response rate of 134 successfully completed questionnaires of a total of 1,059 "expected" responses or a response rate of 12.7 percent. Even as mail surveys go this figure seemed somewhat low. Normally the expected rate of return for mail surveys runs closer to 35 percent to 40 percent. However, upon closer inspection of the data collection process, it appears that the return rate of response is actually much higher than it first appears to be. Indeed, the rate of response relative to the potential initial universe approximates 50 percent and is, therefore, quite acceptable for studies of this type.

Several factors combined to reduce a high response rate. In the first instance, the initial universe of 1,059 respondents was in fact not that large so that any measurements using it as a baseline are misleading. The 1,059 respondents were the number anticipated as an acceptable universe *assuming* that all of the questionnaires provided to the service agencies were forwarded and *assuming* that all the addresses obtained from these agencies were accurate and current. As it turned out neither of these assumptions proved correct. Many of the addresses that were made available were either inaccurate or out of date. In a country as mobile as the United States any respondent who has lived here for five years could be statistically expected to move at least twice. Since the post office keeps forwarding address records for only a six-month period, anyone who had moved even once over the five-year period would most likely not receive a direct mail questionnaire. Moreover, we had no control over the local service agencies. Upon reflection it seems clear that some agencies did send out the questionnaires and some did not. Even when questionnaires were sent by the agencies all too often their own address lists were inaccurate or out-of-date. Finally, the initial requested list required the names of all respondents who were eighteen years old or older in the hope that the sample would include those conscripts who had most recently seen military service. The result of including all people who were eighteen was that a considerable number of respondents included on any list were not yet eighteen when they left the Soviet Union and, therefore, had had no opportunity for military service, and thus the number of individuals who met the survey's requirements was reduced further. Finally, it was noted that although the Soviet conscript system works well, for various reasons approximately 12 percent of eligible Soviet males in fact do not serve. Assuming that the émigré population was representative of the Soviet population as a whole this meant that the initial universe would be reduced by another 12 percent. Taken together these reasons combined to reduce the eligible segments of the original population of 1,059 anticipated respondents by almost 75 percent. Comparative support is found for these figures in the experiences of the researchers of Hebrew University in Baltimore. In a recent attempt to locate émigrés in the Baltimore area, researchers found that over 40 percent of their initial population had moved from their original city addresses in less than a two-year period, a datum that suggests our assumptions about the mobility of the émigré population over a five-year period are accurate.

The probable number of respondents who actually received the survey instrument, all other things equal, was only 265. Of that number, 134 responded, constituting a valid response rate of 50.5 percent of the eligible universe, a response rate well within the valid parameters for any mail survey. Of the 134 initial respondents, 113 reported military service in the Army, and they constitute the core of respondents for this study.

Disregarding, for the moment, the social characteristics of the sample population, which will be addressed later, the question is raised as to how representative the respondents truly are of the Soviet soldier in general and, specifically, in terms of the range of their military experiences. One way of answering that question is to examine the military experience of the sample population in some detail to see whether or not any "lumps" appear in the data. In that way one may discern whether the military experiences of the sample's respondents are representative of what would normally be expected of any soldier in the Soviet Army. There are several indicators of military experience that can be located and examined to analyze the spread of data over the range of alternatives available for each indicator to determine if the military experience of the sample population was in any way idiosyncratic.

One indicator would be to examine the age of the sample population when it first entered military service. The argument might be suggested that because the sample population is comprised largely of Jews who, as a group, have a long tradition of educational achievement, members of this group may not have entered military service at the same time as the control population. If the data on the time of entry into mililtary service are examined, it is found that 73 percent of the sample entered the military between the ages of 18 and 20. Only 7 percent of the sample entered between the ages of 21 and 22, and even this group would not yet have been old enough to have completed a university degree so that an educational deferment for higher university education would have been unlikely. More probable is the explanation that these respondents pursued a course similar to many Soviet young men and entered a two-year technical college. The remaining 20 percent entered the military at the age of 22 or older, suggesting that this group probably did utilize the educational system to defer their entry into the service. It must be pointed out, however, that almost everyone in the Soviet Union eventually serves in the military. Even those who go on to university serve in the reserve forces after a period of active service gained through a program similar to ROTC. Of the 20 percent of the sample who went to university, only 9 percent were able to totally escape active military service, a rate very close to the 12 percent normally expected to avoid military service in the society at large.[1] From the perspective of when the sample population entered military service the data suggest strongly that their military experience was representative of the general Soviet conscript population.

Another way of analyzing the extent to which our sample population is representative of the general Soviet military experience is to determine to what branch of the military respondents were assigned. Were most of them assigned to a particular branch of service or to certain kinds of jobs (perhaps because of their nationality) or, in fact, do they seem to reflect a fairly general spread of military experience across the range of assignment alternatives? If the data in Table A are examined, they reveal a spread of assign-

Table A

Percentage of Respondents Serving in Each Branch of Service

Branch	N	%
Army	66	48.2
Air Force	12	8.7
Navy	13	9.4
Strategic Rockets	6	4.4
Air Defense	17	12.4
Construction	20	14.6
Border Guards	2	1.8
Other	1	.8

ments across the branches of service that indicates a representative spectrum of branch assignments. To be sure, 48.2 percent of the sample served in the army, but since it is the largest service this is not unusual. Some 8.7 percent went into the air force while 9.4 percent went into the navy. Since both services are smaller than the army, the spread of the data once again seems to fall within acceptable parameters. With regard to assignments to Strategic Rocket Forces and Interior Defense Troops, it must be remembered that these units, although technically distinct, really fall under control of the army. Still, the Strategic Rocket Forces, the elite of Soviet military units requiring high technical skills and high level security clearances, absorbed 4.4 percent of the sample population. Air Defense was assigned 12.4 percent and Construction Troops 14.6 percent. The Border Guards, which are generally KGB troops and are comprised of politically reliable people, absorbed 1.5 percent of the sample population while the residual .8 percent were assigned to "other" areas of service. Again, the sample population seems to have served fairly extensively in all branches of the military, suggesting further that their military experiences are generally representative of what we would expect to find in a survey of the Soviet population as a whole.

Looking at the type of military unit respondents served in while in military service one still finds a representative spread across the range of alternatives. An examination of Table B suggests that there is no concentration of sample respondents in any one area that would be particularly divergent from what would be expected—given their level of education and time of entry into service. If anything the number of respondents serving in staff units, 3.5 percent, suggests that their staff experience might be relatively low compared to other groups. The data support the interpretation that sample respondents tended to be heavily concentrated in the combat arms: infantry, artillery, tank, and strategic rocket forces. The 26.5 percent who served in support units is comprised of those who served in *all* types of support units from

Table B

Percentage of Respondents Serving in Types of Army Military Units

Type of Unit	N	%
Infantry	29	25.7
Armor	13	11.5
Artillery	11	9.7
Strategic Rockets	23	20.4
Staff	4	3.5
Support Units	30	26.5
Other	3	2.7

supply companies, chemical battalions, and even political police units. Again, in terms of the type of military units in which the sample respondents served, they appear to have a typical profile of military experience with a slight imbalance toward service in the combat arms.

One of the more accurate indicators of the degree to which the sample population's military experience is representative of Soviet military experience is the extent to which its members attained a rank above that of general soldier or private. If the sample is examined, it demonstrates that the sample population accurately represents the Soviet Army as a whole. For example, 52.2 percent of the sample served only as general soldiers or privates, a very normal percentage. Well over half remained in service for their initial two or three year tour of duty, depending upon time of entry, and never rose above the rank of private. Fully 26.5 percent rose to the rank of noncommissioned officer, implying that the rate of military upward mobility in the sample is relatively normal. Using the figure of about 25 percent of total forces serving as noncommissioned officers in the American army, the 26.5 percent noncommissioned officers in the sample seems fairly representative of that percentage of force strength normally allocated to these ranks. In general, Soviet noncommissioned officer strength is somewhat higher than the strength of similar ranks in the American army although no exact figures exist. Soviet numbers are higher precisely because they do not have a professional, stable noncommissioned officer corps and try to make up the qualitative difference with increased numbers of noncommissioned ranks to carry out supervisory and command tasks. The 26.5 percent of the sample respondents who reached the rank of noncommissioned officer falls between the 25 percent and 28 percent of the Soviet Army strength that would normally be allotted to noncommissioned officers. The number of warrant officers in the sample is 2.7 percent. It is unclear whether or not this figure is representative of overall Soviet strength at this rank level because the warrant officer program began only five years ago and the data on the number of warrant officers relative to other ranks are unavailable.

The data indicate that 17.7 percent of the sample respondents reached officer rank. Once again this figure seems to be generally aligned with what the normal officer strength profile of the Soviet Army actually is. Estimates vary, but at least 15 percent of Soviet military strength is considered to be comprised of officers and some estimates are as high as 18 percent. The figures go even higher if one counts warrant officers and young ensigns. Regardless of what estimates are used it still seems clear that the rate at which the sample respondents attained officer status, some 17.7 percent of the total sample, is well within normal parameters. Certainly there is no evidence that the sample population was prohibited from attaining its "fair share" of officers.

Still another indicator of the degree to which the sample reflects the typical military experiences of Soviet soldiers is found in the number of respondents who reached command and supervisory positions at either enlisted or officer levels. Five analytical categories were developed: those who held command enlisted positions such as squad leaders, platoon sergeants, and company sergeants; those who held supervisory enlisted positions largely in staff units, support units, or headquarters command units; those who were commanding officers, that is, platoon leaders, company commanders, battery commanders, missile launch commanders, and so on; and those officers who held supervisory positions in staff and support units. The residual category is comprised of those who held neither command nor supervisory positions regardless of rank. Stratifying on these categories of analysis the data clearly indicate that the profile of the sample coincides closely with what we would expect for any group of soldiers chosen at random. Some 15.9 percent of the sample population held command positions at the enlisted level while 14.2 percent held supervisory positions at the same level, Surprisingly, 10.6 percent of the sample held command positions at the officer level, somewhat higher than expected. However, if this figure is combined with the number of officers who held supervisory posts (8.0 percent) the resulting figure is 18.6 percent or approximately the normal percentage of officers estimated in the Soviet Army. To be sure, the largest residual category, 51.3 percent, held neither enlisted nor officer supervisory or command positons, as expected. Thus, from the perspective of achieving command roles within the Soviet Army, sample respondents appear generally congruent with the norm.

A final indicator would be to examine the periods of service of the sample population. It might be argued that respondents emigrated to the West because of their disenchantment with the Soviet system. If this is the case, it could be suggested that these respondents *ab initio* do not accurately reflect the true attitudes of the bulk of Soviet soldiers who, after all, did not emigrate. While this problem will be addressed in detail later, the question of émigré status as being alienative of one's military views would make sense only if the sample population knew they were going to emigrate at the time they served in the military. Since the relaxed emigration policy is less than seven years old, all of the respondents who served prior to 1973 could hardly have anticipated they would emigrate; in which case, it is unlikely that their views or their experiences in the military were affected by the anticipation of emigration.

To discover just how accurate or how wide a spectrum of military service the sample represents we can focus upon when the respondents served in the military. The sample spans a period of military service beginning prior to World War II and ending as late as 1978. Thus, 4.4 percent of the respondents served in the prewar army while 21.2 percent served during the war years and in the immediate postwar period. Some 18.6 percent served in the early post-Stalin era from 1953 through 1957 and 11.5 percent served between 1958 and 1963, a period that witnessed the Cuban missile crisis. Finally, 44.2 percent of the respondents served in the modern Soviet Army between 1964 and 1978. Only 11.5 percent of the respondents saw military service between 1973 and 1978, the period in which an awareness of the real possibility of emigration may have affected their perceptions of military service. At the very worst, slightly more than 10 percent of the respondents *may* have had their views biased by anticipating emigration. There is no valid way to confirm this, however; only the possibility of bias can be raised. In respect to their overall range of service, however, the sample represents a span of some forty years of military service providing a crucial background variable against which other dimensions of the data can be analyzed.

The point of analysis is to suggest that when sample respondents are stratified along several dimensions of the data it appears that their range of military service is about as close as possible to that which we would typically expect to find among any randomly selected group of conscripts in the Soviet Army. Our respondents entered military service at the same time any Soviet soldier would and they served in different branches of the military at about the same rate as any group. Within the army itself, they served in its different branches at normal rates and in terms of their ability to rise to levels of command, they seem very close to the overall norm. The same seems true when their time range of military service is examined and certainly in terms of the levels of rank they eventually attained. From the perspective of their overall military experience the sample population upon which this study rests seems an accurate microcosm of the typical experience of the Soviet soldier. Where it does diverge the points of difference are minimal, indeed, insignificant compared to the major thrust of the data. It seems safe, therefore, to assume that from the perspective of their military service the views and feelings of respondents generally reflect the views and feelings of any randomly selected group of conscripts in the Soviet Army. Further, given the time span over which respondents saw military service, this degree of reliability can be assumed to apply at any point in time upon which this analysis chooses to focus.

Given that the sample is accurately representative of the experiences of the Soviet conscript, it is appropriate to focus upon a question that inevitably goes to the heart of the study. That question concerns the fact that the bulk of the respondents are Jews. The argument is raised that as the respondents are Jews they might be outside the mainstream of Soviet life and, accordingly, their views of the Soviet military may be biased. It can be suggested further that the respondents' status as émigrés necessarily implies a high degree of social alienation that also would bias their views. How valid are these questions, and how can they be answered?

One response to the problem of bias is to suggest that if the sample is biased then an examination of the pages and pages of raw data should reveal the presence of certain "lumps" among the response profiles of certain questions. Accordingly, such an examination must show that the data are biased in the same direction if the argument is to have merit. A thorough examination of the data across 161 variables reveals no particularly extreme bulges. By and large respondents tend to spread rather "normally" in a statistical sense throughout the range of questions indicating that their responses are as "normal" as could be expected from any randomly selected sample. In any case only one of two positions in such a statistical analysis is acceptable: one assumes that either a sample of Jewish émigrés is biased in the direction of a negative view of the Soviet Army or it is biased in the direction of a positive view. The only other alternatives are that the data are unbiased or randomly distributed. Given the spread of the data in which no statistically significant lumps appear, one is hard pressed from either position to explain both the very positive *and* very negative things respondents say about the Soviet Army. If it is assumed that bias is negative, then positive responses cannot be logically explained. The reverse is also true. The only other alternatives are to affirm that the data are not biased or else to affirm that the responses are randomly distributed. In any case, an analysis of the data for statistical "lumps" does not reveal any meaningful idiosyncrasies. It most certainly does not reveal consistent statistical bias along any discernible dimension.

Another response to the argument that the sample is biased is to suggest that émigré status per se does not *ab initio* bias the sample. Historically, the desire to emigrate has been largely a result of the availability of the opportunity to do so. Since 1972 the only people who have been allowed to emigrate from the Soviet Union have been Jews. Accordingly, they have emigrated! To be sure this says little about whether or not they are alienated from that society or the degree of such alienation. It suggests only that the opportunity to leave provides a person or a group with one more option to exercise in a fairly oppressive society. In hundreds of personal conversations with émigrés, this analyst found none of the vitriolic hatred of the regime that one would expect. A more commonly voiced sentiment is a deep sense of disappointment that the Soviet regime has been unable to live up to the great ideals it professes. This was especially the case among well-educated respondents. I could find no particularly strong ideological disagreement. By and large the respondents' assessment of life in the Soviet Union is patently lacking in ideological content. The impression is that émigré status per se does not overtly cast a bias in the data largely because it is difficult to locate any particular ideological reason for leaving.

Among sample respondents it is very difficult to find people who left because they felt they were being persecuted as Jews; nor is it common to find people who left because they feared for their lives or feared that their children would be wooed away from their Jewish heritage by an atheistic regime. One finds even fewer respondents who left out of burning ideological attachment to the West, a point brought out by the fact that a measurable number of émigrés, especially to Israel, actually return to the Soviet Union. The picture of ideologically committed dissidents so commonly portrayed in the West is simply not an accurate description of the mass of Soviet émigrés. Indeed, some respondents even expressed the view that such dissidents were either crazy or dangerous.

By and large one finds people leaving Russia for the reasons people have always left countries—the search for better opportunities for themselves and their children. Scores of indepth interviews with respondents suggest that leaving Russia was not so much a result of being antiregime, certainly not anticommunist, and not a fear of being killed or having their children lose their sense of Jewish identity, as much as it was simply a desire to improve one's quality of life coupled with the realization that the opportunity to emigrate might be suddenly closed off. Emigration from the Soviet Union does not appear to be the sociological and psychological equivalent of, say, emigration from Germany in the 1930s, when people fled in fear for their lives. Nor does it appear to be the equivalent of emigration from the United States to Canada during the Vietnam War, which was basically provoked by ideological differences. More likely, it seems to be the kind of emigration that one witnesses for example in Ireland or England where the leaving of one's homeland is largely a result of the opportunity to emigrate and the search for a better life. From this perspective—buttressed by a large number of conversations with émigrés—it does not appear that being an émigré necessarily prohibits presenting an accurate accounting of past experiences in military service. Certainly it does not bias the data provided by those respondents who had accomplished their military service before the possibility of emigration ever became a reality.

The argument may still be raised that because most respondents are Jews they were outside the mainstream of Soviet society and, as such, their relative social position biases their perceptions of their military experience. The question resolves itself to the following terms: Is being Jewish, in itself, a bias in terms of the experiences one is likely to have in the Soviet military? One way of addressing this question is to investigate the degree to which the Soviet Jew resides outside the mainstream of Soviet society, if indeed he does at all, and then to examine to what extent the sample is truly representative of Soviet Jewry in general.

Addressing the second question first it would seem that the sample is fairly representative of the general Jewish population in the Soviet Union. For example, the data indicate that 92.9 percent of the respondents come from urban areas. The *Handbook of Major Soviet Nationalities* notes that 97.8 percent of the Jewish population in Russia resides in urban areas.[2] In terms of rural backgrounds about 7.1 percent of the sample comes from small towns or villages compared to about 3.5 percent of the general Jewish population in the Soviet Union. The sample seems relatively accurate in terms of the urban-rural residence variable. The data reflect a similar situation in terms of education. In educational achievement, the sample is fairly close to what we would expect to find among Jews in the Soviet Union. Some 11.5 percent of the sample had college degrees compared to only 9.0 percent for the Russian populace as a whole. This confirms the general tendency in the Soviet Union for Jews to be better educated than other Russian groups.[3] Taken together, the data support the proposition that in terms of urban residence and educational achievement, the sample is not seriously divergent from the Russian Jewish population. Moreover, in general terms it seems that Soviet Jews are only marginally and insignificantly divergent from the mainstream of Soviet life. Regardless of whether or not being Jewish biases one's opinions on military service, it seems clear that the sample is at least an accurate portrait of the Russian Jewish population.

The question still to be addressed is whether or not being Jewish places a person outside the mainstream of Soviet life. If Jews are outside the mainstream of Soviet society, it can be argued that their perceptions are likely to be biased. On the other hand, if Soviet Jews are not outside the general tenor of Soviet life then it can be argued that their views of military life are generally representative of *any* randomly selected group within the Soviet Army.

It must be rememberd that the Soviet Union is a multinational state comprised of a host of nationality groups, some of which see themselves as being forcibly held within the borders of the Soviet empire. In such a society the ideal way to obtain a valid view of how things are would be to conduct a large cross-sectional study. Such an effort is of course impossible in light of the obvious limitations imposed by the Soviet regime. Soviet authorities are unwilling to cooperate in terms of allowing these kinds of studies. As Malenkov once said of Soviet objections to free elections, one never knows how they are going to turn out. The same may be said of the Soviet attitude toward "unguided" research efforts. Accordingly, the researcher is forced to confront two alternatives, neither an ideal solution to the problem. The researcher can choose to study only one group, say Ukrainians, but then is open to the charge that this one group is not representative of the society as a whole; therefore, the conclusions are suspect. On the other hand, if the researcher chooses to study only the Great Russian population he is inevitably forced to ignore the national groups that comprise approximately 49 percent of the population of the Soviet state and comprise at least 49 percent of its military conscripts. Here the researcher will be charged with biasing the data in the other direction, namely, that at least half the groups in Soviet society are ignored by this methodology. Is there a solution to the dilemma?

One solution, although not ideal but workable, is to examine a group that is truly a national group in its own right and thus reflects many of the attitudes that nationalities are likely to feel while at the same time studying a group that is very much assimilated into the dominant Russian culture so that it reflects many of the views of the dominant culture. As an alternative to a completely comprehensive survey, the examination of such a group should produce a fairly accurate portrait of not only Russian views but also the views of nationality groups. The group would constitute a composite perspective that a researcher could uncover in a random survey of any social institution that draws representatively from all sections of Soviet society as does the Soviet Army. Russian Jews comprise just such a group. On the one hand they are clearly a minority national group, a fact that needs no proof beyond a cursory reading of Russian history, and yet they appear the closest of all national groups to the Russian mainstream.

That the Jews are the most assimilated of all the Soviet Union's national groups is beyond question. In terms of language, for example, in 1970 fully 82.3 percent of Russian Jews listed Russian as their mother tongue, the highest rate of all national groups. Fully 94.5 percent listed themselves as fluent in Russian as either a first or second language.[4] Linguistically, they are by far the most assimilated group. Another indicator of assimilation into the Russian mainstream is intermarriage. Such data are somewhat sketchy but estimates are that intermarriage may be as high as 35 percent among all age groups of Russian-Jewish youth, again the highest rate of intermarriage of all national groups.[5] With intermarriage comes a tendency to reject past Jewish ties and to overtly identify with predominant Russian ones. An official Soviet report notes too that the children of mixed couples "usually choose that nationality, that language and culture with which they are most familiar."[6] Generally speaking this means that Jews in the Soviet Union are moving further and further into the Russian social mainstream and in fact have been doing so for over a hundred years.

A third indicator of the degree of Jewish assimilation into the Russian
societal mainstream can be gauged from the fact that Jews have historically
remained loyal to the Russian state when other groups like Ukrainians or
Estonians have taken up arms against it or even welcomed foreign invaders.
Unlike other national groups, Jews did not desert in large numbers during
World War II. They remained loyal to the Soviet state and this loyalty
clearly extended to their contributions in military service. As Katz has
pointed out in his study, "Jews fought bravely in World War II compiling
one of the highest ratios of Heroes of the Soviet Union among all nationality
groups."[7] Clearly, one of the reasons why Jews have been awash in the
Soviet social mainstream is precisely because they do not have a national
homeland that they perceive as occupied by the Russian state as do other
national groups.

The process of assimilation for Jews has been helped by the fact that unlike
other national groups within the Soviet Union the Jews do not possess a
national language of their own. Russian is spoken almost exclusively; Hebrew
seems to be either a dead language or reserved largely for religious cere-
monies. Moreover, they lack national customs of their own and as a result
their assimilation has been speeded perhaps because of the lack of meaningful alternatives. Even religious ties are weak, and there is little organized
religious practice in the Soviet Union. What religious instruction there is
and what religious services are held seem to attract mostly people over fifty,
the young having turned from Judaism as a cultural force. This is reflected
in reports compiled by HIAS, the Hebrew Immigrant Aid Society, which is
largely responsible for the movement of Soviet Jews to the West. HIAS
notes that Soviet Jews often know little of Judaism, that most are not practi-
cing Jews, that they lack knowledge of key religious rituals, and that for most
purposes they are more Russian than Jewish.[8] The impression is strong that
as a religio-cultural force Judaism appears very weak. Moreover, the set-
tlement patterns of the Jews in Russia are such that the community is both
historically and linguistically fragmented. In terms of social history, one
can discern at least four basic kinds of "Jewish peoples" in the Soviet Union
and most are virtually unrecognizable to one another. In a sense, the Jews
are among the most heterogeneous of national groups and from this racio-
cultural perspective, there is very little to bond them together.

Taken together it would seem that Jews in the Soviet Union are not forged
together by strong religious ties, are not held together as other groups by
the perception of a shared but conquered homeland, and are not welded together by common national language and custom. As a result they are, by
all indicators, very assimilated and far more Russian than they are Jewish. At
the same time that they are firmly within the Russian mainstream they remain
a distinct nationality group, if for no reason other than that they are thought
of as such by other national groups and because it is official Soviet policy to
treat them as such. Their unique position makes them valuable observers

since they bring to bear the perspectives of both Russians and the nationalities on their military experiences. Accordingly, an examination of their views produces a valid sample of representative opinions without having to conduct a large, multi-ethnic sample—an impossible task under existing conditions. The position of Jews as participant-observers makes them accurately representative of the perspectives found within Soviet multinational institutions such as the Soviet Army. They are different enough from the Russians to adequately reflect nationality sentiments while being different enough from the nationalities to accurately portray Russian sentiments. As such they comprise a composite social psychology which suggests their views are as accurate and representative of those attitudes and views as we could find within any large group of Soviet conscripts selected at random.

The thrust of the argument thus far has been to suggest that one can learn about the Soviet Army by talking to its soldiers and that much can be learned about the Soviet military by examining the attitudes and experiences of those who have served in it. This argument would be accepted unquestionably if it were possible to conduct a systematic empirical survey of all the different groups within the Soviet Union. Since this is not possible, having to use a group of respondents because they are available undoubtedly will raise questions as to the validity of their perceptions. I have tried to suggest that neither émigré status nor being Jewish removes members of this group from consideration as valid observers of their own military experience. In the end there is no way to eliminate all bias in any sample. However, one can point to the previous arguments as well as to the statistical analysis of the data to suggest that whatever biases are extant, they are not debilitating. The ground is firm enough to support the assumption that the data are generally accurate.

In the final analysis, it is clear that this study represents the only extant systematic empirical examination of attitudes and experiences of Soviet soldiers undertaken since 1947. However, no claim is offered that the study is definitive, or that the data are totally free from error, or that the resulting conclusions are necessarily to be accepted without question. The only claim put forth for the data is that they are available, systematic, empirical, generally representative, largely reliable, and above all useful. Until the Soviet authorities allow social scientists to undertake studies of Soviet soldiers within the country—something even Western democracies often find difficult to allow—the available data will have to suffice.

Within these pages researchers will find the means to reconstruct the entire body of data for use on their own computers so as to undertake further analysis. Chapters 2 and 3 contain the complete questionnaire and codebook; the codebook has been further annotated with a six-character codeword for every question entry. Chapters 4 and 5 include a list of two hundred and twenty-seven data tables that have been extracted from the material. A complete frequency listing for each question in the survey is provided as well as some one hundred cross-tabulations of variables and relationships that were believed most important. Chapter 6 contains the raw data files in numeric form—one hundred and thirteen files—each set of numbers corresponding to one completed interview. The researcher has but to enter them on computer tape using the provided code manual as a guide. An extensive and up-to-date bibliography of available source materials dealing with the Soviet soldier completes the book. A substantial number of these sources have been extracted from Soviet press and military periodicals. It contains almost all of the current relevant unclassified material available.

In the end, of course, students of the subject must go where their intuition and interpretation of the available data lead them. By making this data widely available to the academic community it is hoped that insight will be sharpened, intuition tested, old hypotheses disproven, and new ones generated. In themselves data are never a substitute for "flashes of insight." But they can help generate and test the brightness and accuracy of such flashes. That is the hope I have for this work.

NOTES

1. This figure is one usually used by the American intelligence community in assessing the extent of Soviet nonparticipation in military service. It is clearly an estimate.

2. Zev Katz, Rosemarie Rogers, and Frederic Harned, *Handbook of Major Soviet Nationalities* (New York: Free Press, 1975), p. 357.

3. *Ibid.*, p. 376.

4. *Ibid.*, p. 371.

5. *Ibid.*, p. 380.

6. *Literary Gazette*, January 24, 1973, p. 13.

7. Katz, Rogers, and Harned, *Handbook*, p. 363.

8. "Fact Sheet on Russian Resettlement Program," HIAS report, January 1978.

The
Questionnaire _____

OPINION RESEARCH CENTER
MANCHESTER, NEW HAMPSHIRE

INSTRUCTIONS:

This questionnaire is designed to obtain your views about your experiences in military service. All answers are confidential and no identification of respondents is possible. Answer all questions as truthfully as possible. There are no right or wrong answers. What is important is your opinions and views about your personal experiences.

1. How old are you now? _____

2. How old were you when you first went into military service? _____

3. How long did you stay in military service?

    1.( ) under one year
    2.( ) one year
    3.( ) less than two years
    4.( ) two years
    5.( ) more than two years (How many years? _____)

4. When were you in military service?

    From _____ To _____ (Years only)

5. What type of living area did you come from before you entered the military?

    1.( ) small rural village
    2.( ) small urban town
    3.( ) large city
    4.( ) medium size city

6. What was the highest level of education you achieved <u>before</u> you went into the military?

_____

7. Did you obtain more education <u>after</u> you left military service?

    1.( ) Yes 2.( ) No

8. Did you learn any useful civilian skills while you were in the military?

    1.( ) Yes 2.( ) No

9. What part of the military were you in?

    1.( ) army
    2.( ) air force
    3.( ) navy
    4.( ) strategic rocket forces
    5.( ) air defense corps
    6.( ) construction troops
    7.( ) border guards
    8.( ) other: _____(specify)

10. What was the highest rank you attained?

    1.( ) private soldier
    2.( ) non-commissioned
    3.( ) warrant officer
    4.( ) officer

11. What was your actual rank title? _____

12. What type of military unit were you in?

    1.( ) infantry
    2.( ) tanks
    3.( ) artillery
    4.( ) rockets
    5.( ) rear support unit
    6.( ) staff unit
    7.( ) other:_____(specify)

13. Did you make any close friends while you were
    in the military?

    1.( ) Yes   2.( ) No

14. About how many close friends did you have in
    the military?

    1.( ) one
    2.( ) two
    3.( ) three
    4.( ) four
    5.( ) five
    6.( ) six or more

15. In general was your service in the military a
    pleasant or unpleasant experience?

    1.( ) pleasant
    2.( ) unpleasant

16. If you could have avoided going into the mili-
    tary like some people did, would you have
    avoided it?

    1.( ) Yes   2.( ) No

17. How did your family feel about your going into
    the military?

    1.( ) thought it was my duty
    2.( ) thought it was a good thing
    3.( ) were generally not happy with my going
    4.( ) had no real feeling about it
    5.( ) resigned because it could not be avoided
    6.( ) were proud that I was serving my country

18. Did your friends think that going into the mili-
    tary was a good thing, something to be proud of,
    or something that could not be avoided?

    1.( ) a good thing
    2.( ) something to be proud of
    3.( ) something that could not be avoided

19. At the time you were in the military did you
    think that it was a waste of time?

    1.( ) Yes   2.( ) No

20. Do you think you got anything good out of
    going in the military?

    1.( ) Yes   2.( ) No

21. Was military life more difficult than you
    expected?

    1.( ) Yes   2.( ) No

22. About how much free time did you have to your-
    self in an average week?

    1.( ) only a few hours
    2.( ) about a day
    3.( ) almost none at all
    4.( ) every minute was accounted for
    5.( ) generally enough free time

23. Compared to what you were being paid before you
    went into the military, was military pay more
    or less?

    1.( ) less   2.( ) more

24. Was your pay enough for your needs?

    1.( ) Yes   2.( ) No

25. Did your family ever have to send you money
    so that you could get by?

    1.( ) Yes   2.( ) No

26. Was hot water available every day for showers in your military unit?

    1.( ) Yes   2.( ) No

27. Was the food in the military generally better or worse than in civilian life?

    1.( ) better
    2.( ) worse
    3.( ) about the same

28. Was the quality of food you received adequate?

    1.( ) Yes   2.( ) No

29. Was the amount of food you received adequate for your needs?

    1.( ) Yes   2.( ) No

30. In general, how would you describe the living quarters you lived in while in the military?

    1.( ) very good
    2.( ) good
    3.( ) adequate
    4.( ) poor
    5.( ) bad
    6.( ) very bad

31. In your experience was housing in the military generally better than what you were used to in civilian life?

    1.( ) Yes   2.( ) No

32. Were the toilets located inside the barracks or was it necessary to go outside?

    1.( ) inside
    2.( ) outside

33. Were the barracks normally warm enough in winter to keep you comfortable?

    1.( ) Yes   2.( ) No

34. Did anyone in your unit ever develop sores or carbuncles from having a poor diet?

    1.( ) Yes   2.( ) No

35. Did anyone in your unit ever develop any other illness because of improper or inadequate diet?

    1.( ) Yes   2.( ) No

36. How much did the troops complain about the food?

    1.( ) very much
    2.( ) often
    3.( ) seldom
    4.( ) rarely
    5.( ) almost never

37. Did you or anyone in your unit ever obtain extra food from sources outside the military?

    1.( ) Yes   2.( ) No

38. Was this a common practice?

    1.( ) Yes   2.( ) No

39. Did you ever hear of anyone in your unit selling state property to get some extra money?

    1.( ) Yes   2.( ) No

40. Were the troop barracks usually overcrowded?

    1.( ) Yes   2.( ) No

41. Was this the usual condition in most units that you know of?

    1.( ) Yes   2.( ) No

42. In your unit about how many soldiers lived in a single room?

    _____(specify number)

43. About how many square meters was the room? _____

44. Did you have enough space and privacy in your barracks?

    1.( ) Yes   2.( ) No

45. Is the lack of privacy and space a major complaint among the soldiers?

    1.( ) Yes   2.( ) No

46. Does this lack of space or privacy lead to frequent fights among the soldiers?

    1.( ) Yes   2.( ) No

47. Could you make some extra money in the military by trading or selling things to other soldiers or to civilians?

    1.( ) Yes   2.( ) No

48. While you were in the military were you able to save some money for when you returned to civilian life?

    1.( ) Yes   2.( ) No

49. In general how much did the troops complain about the pay they received?

    1.( ) very much
    2.( ) often
    3.( ) seldom
    4.( ) rarely
    5.( ) almost never

50. Did you ever hear stories about soldiers who were forced to give some of their pay to other soldiers or to non-commissioned officers?

    1.( ) Yes   2.( ) No

51. In the whole time you were in the military, how many times were you allowed to leave the base for your own recreation?

    _____(number of times)

52. Were you ever allowed to leave the base without the company of some higher ranking soldier to keep an eye on things?

    1.( ) Yes   2.( ) No

53. How many times? _____

54. During your time in the military were you able to meet women?

    1.( ) Yes   2.( ) No

55. How often did you get to meet women?

    1.( ) very often
    2.( ) often
    3.( ) seldom
    4.( ) rarely
    5.( ) almost never

56. Could you visit these women in places off the military base?

    1.( ) Yes   2.( ) No

57. Did soldiers have to leave the base without permission to see women?

58. How often did soldiers in your unit leave the base without permission to see women?

    1.( ) very often
    2.( ) often
    3.( ) seldom
    4.( ) rarely
    5.( ) almost never

59. If you were caught leaving the base without permission to visit a woman was the punishment generally harsh or lenient?

    1.( ) harsh
    2.( ) lenient

60. Did anyone in your unit ever physically assault an officer?

    1.( ) Yes   2.( ) No

61. Did anyone in your unit ever physically assault a non-commissioned officer?

    1.( ) Yes   2.( ) No

62. Did anyone in your unit ever physically assault a warrant officer?

    1.( ) Yes   2.( ) No

63. Have you heard stories about other units where officers have been assaulted?

    1.( ) Yes   2.( ) No

64. In your opinion, how well do you think your unit would have fought in actual combat.

    1.( ) very well
    2.( ) fairly well
    3.( ) moderately well
    4.( ) poorly
    5.( ) very poorly

65. Did your officers seem to care very much about the morale of your unit?

    1.( ) Yes   2.( ) No

66. In your experience would you say that soldiers drink more in the military than in civilian life?

    1.( ) more in the military
    2.( ) more in the civilian life

67. Do officers drink heavily?

    1.( ) Yes   2.( ) No

68. Did you ever hear of or see an officer drunk on duty?

    1.( ) Yes   2.( ) No

69. Did you ever hear of or see a non-commissioned officer drunk on duty?

    1.( ) Yes   2.( ) No

70. How often are ordinary soldiers drinking or drunk while on duty?

    1.( ) very often
    2.( ) often
    3.( ) seldom
    4.( ) rarely
    5.( ) almost never

71. Do superior officers regard excessive drinking as a major problem in the military?

    1.( ) Yes   2.( ) No

72. Did the amount of drinking in your unit affect the ability of your unit to perform its mission?

    1.( ) Yes   2.( ) No   3.( ) Probably did

73. Are the punishments for drinking on duty severe
    or generally lenient?

    1.( ) severe
    2.( ) lenient

74. In your experience in the military were cer-
    tain national and religious groups singled out
    for unfair treatment?

    1.( ) Yes   2.( ) No

75. Was this a common practice?

    1.( ) Yes   2.( ) No

76. How often do more experienced soldiers treat
    new recruits unfairly?

    1.( ) very often
    2.( ) often
    3.( ) seldom
    4.( ) rarely
    5.( ) almost never

77. Does this have a negative effect on the soldiers
    morale?

    1.( ) Yes   2.( ) No

78. Are the officers aware of the unfair treat-
    ment that soldiers receive from other older
    soldiers?

    1.( ) Yes   2.( ) No

79. How often so sargeants treat the troops un-
    fairly?

    1.( ) very often
    2.( ) often
    3.( ) seldom
    4.( ) rarely
    5.( ) almost never

80. In general do soldiers feel that they can go
    to their officers or sargeants with a com-
    plaint about being treated unfairly?

    1.( ) Yes   2.( ) No

81. Generally do most civilians treat soldiers well
    when the soldier is away from his base?

    1.( ) Yes   2.( ) No

82. In your opinion, how important do you think
    that belief in an ideology--Marxism-Leninism--
    is in motivating a soldier to fight well?

    1.( ) the most important factor
    2.( ) a very important factor
    3.( ) not very important at all
    4.( ) almost totally unimportant

83. Which of the following things do you think is
    most important to motivating a soldier to fight
    well? (CHOOSE ONLY ONE)

    1.( ) close ties to his comrades in the unit
    2.( ) support of the friends back home
    3.( ) feeling that one's officers/nco's care
          about you
    4.( ) belief in an ideology
    5.( ) not wanting to appear a coward in front
          of your friends

84. When you were in the military did anyone in
    your unit ever commit suicide?

    1.( )Yes   2.( ) No

85. Did anyone in your unit ever attempt to com-
    mit suicide?

    1.( ) Yes   2.( ) No

86. Did you ever hear stories about people com-
    mitting suicide in other units?

    1.( ) Yes   2.( ) No

87. How common were the stories about suicide and
    suicide attempts?

    1.( ) very common
    2.( ) common
    3.( ) generally uncommon
    4.( ) fairly rare
    5.( ) almost never

88. In your experience whenever you heard about
    suicide in the military did it happen most when:

    1.( ) the soldier first came into the army
    2.( ) after he had been with his unit for awhile

89. Whenever you heard stories about suicide or su-
    icide attempts, were there stories about officers
    as well?

    1.( ) Yes   2.( ) No

90. Non-commissioned officers?

    1.( ) Yes   2.( ) No

91. Warrant officers?

    1.( ) Yes   2.( ) No

92. Is it true that many suicide attempts are actually attempts to get a release from military service?

    1.( ) Yes   2.( ) No

93. In your experience, were your superiors concerned about the problem of suicide?

    1.( ) Yes   2.( ) No

94. In your unit how many conscript nco's did you have?

    _____

95. How many professional nco's did you have?

    _____

96. How many officers? _____

97. How many warrant officers? _____

98. Given the general quality of officers that you served with in your military service, how would you rate their quality as officers?

    1.( ) extremely good
    2.( ) good
    3.( ) average
    4.( ) fair
    5.( ) poor
    6.( ) very poor

99. How would you rate the quality of the non-commissioned officers you came into contact with?

    1.( ) extremely good
    2.( ) good
    3.( ) average
    4.( ) fair
    5.( ) poor
    6.( ) very poor

100. How close to your fellow soldiers did you feel when you were in the military?

    1.( ) very close
    2.( ) close
    3.( ) moderately close
    4.( ) not close at all
    5.( ) I felt few bonds with them

101. How strongly did you develop feelings of pride and affection for your military unit?

    1.( ) very strongly
    2.( ) strongly
    3.( ) moderately
    4.( ) not very strong
    5.( ) unit pride did not concern me much
    6.( ) no feelings of pride at all

102. When you were in the military did anyone in your unit ever desert?

    1.( ) Yes   2.( ) No

103. Did you ever hear of an officer deserting?

    1.( ) Yes   2.( ) No

104. Did you ever hear of a warrant officer deserting?

    1.( ) Yes   2.( ) No

105. Did you ever hear of a non-commissioned officer deserting?

    1.( ) Yes 2.( ) No

106. In general, were the stories that you heard about soldiers deserting,

    1.( ) very common
    2.( ) common
    3.( ) generally uncommon
    4.( ) rare
    5.( ) almost never heard such stories

107. How often did soldiers in your unit go absent without leave?

    1.( ) quite often
    2.( ) often
    3.( ) fairly often
    4.( ) not very much
    5.( ) rarely
    6.( ) almost never

108. What are some of the reasons that soldiers tried to go absent without leave? (check three of the most common reasons).

1.( ) to get vodka
2.( ) to meet women
3.( ) to escape military life for a short time
4.( ) to try to get away from the military for good
5.( ) family problems
6.( ) unfair treatment by superiors
7.( ) to buy some extra food
8.( ) to get some drugs

109. Were your superiors concerned with the problem of soldiers going absent without leave?

1.( ) Yes   2.( ) No

110. Were they concerned about the problem of desertion?

1.( ) Yes   2.( ) No

111. In general, is going absent without leave a big problem in the military?

1.( ) Yes
2.( ) No

112. Is desertion a big problem in the military?

1.( ) Yes
2.( ) No

113. Is the punishment for going absent without leave harsh or lenient?

1.( ) harsh
2.( ) lenient

Below are a series of statements that people have
used to describe their officers, non-commissioned officers, and warrant officers. As you read each statement, if you agree that it describes the officers you
knew, place a mark in the space marked "officers." If
it describes the non-commissioned officers you knew, mark
the space "non-commissioned officers" and if it describes
the warrant officers you knew, mark the space "warrant officers." If it describes all three types of superiors,
mark the space "all three". If the statement does not
describe any of your superiors, mark the space "not
applicable".

---

114. Was genuinely interested in his men's personal
     problems.

     1.( ) officer   5.( ) not applicable
     2.( ) non-commissioned officer
     3.( ) warrant officer
     4.( ) all three

115. Went out of his way to show an interest in his men.

     1.( ) officer   5.( ) not applicable
     2.( ) non-commissioned officer
     3.( ) warrant officer
     4.( ) all three

116. Seemed more concerned with his own career advance-
     ment than with his men.

     1.( ) officer   5.( ) not applicable
     2.( ) non-commissioned officer
     3.( ) warrant officer
     4.( ) all three

117. He treated people in an impersonal manner-- like cogs
     in a machine.

     1.( ) officer   5.( ) not applicable
     2.( ) non-commissioned officer
     3.( ) warrant officer
     4.( ) all three

118. Stood up for his men when dealing with his superiors.

     1.( ) officer   5.( ) not applicable
     2.( ) non-commissioned officer
     3.( ) warrant officer
     4.( ) all three

119. Criticised subordinates in front of others.

    1.( ) officers   5.( ) not applicable
    2.( ) non-commissioned officers
    3.( ) warrant officers
    4.( ) all three

120. Shared hardships with his troops.

    1.( ) officers   5.( ) not applicable
    2.( ) non-commissioned officers
    3.( ) warrant officers
    4.( ) all three

121.   Saw to it that his men had the things they needed in military life.

    1.( ) officers   5.( ) not applicable
    2.( ) non-commissioned officers
    3.( ) warrant officers
    4.( ) all three

122. Always set the example for his men.

    1.( ) officers   5.( ) not applicable
    2.( ) non-commissioned officers
    3.( ) warrant officers
    4.( ) all three

123. Drew too strong a line between himself and his men; he was too distant.

    1.( ) officers   5.( ) not applicable
    2.( ) non-commissioned officers
    3.( ) warrant officers
    4.( ) all three

124. Had the kind of judgement I would trust in combat.

    1.( ) officers   5.( ) not applicable
    2.( ) non-commissioned officers
    3.( ) warrant officers
    4.( ) all three

125. Truly knew his men and respected their capabilities.

    1.( ) officers   5.( ) not applicable
    2.( ) non-commissioned officers
    3.( ) warrant officers
    4.( ) all three

126. Never developed close personal ties with his men.

1.( ) officers   5.( ) not applicable
2.( ) non-commissioned officers
3.( ) warrant officers
4.( ) all three

127. He was concerned about the unit's morale and did everything he could to make it high.

1.( ) officers   5.( ) not applicable
2.( ) non-commissioned officers
3.( ) warrant officers
4.( ) all three

128. Often tried to avoid taking responsibility when
things went wrong.

1.( ) officers   5.( ) not applicable
2.( ) non-commissioned officers
3.( ) warrant officers
4.( ) all three

129. Listened with genuine sympathy to the problems of
the troops.

1.( ) officers   5.( ) not applicable
2.( ) non-commissioned officers
3.( ) warrant officers
4.( ) all three

130. Often praised his troops for doing a good job and
meant it.

1.( ) officers   5.( ) not applicable
2.( ) non-commissioned officers
3.( ) warrant officers
4.( ) all three

131. Would make a good man to go into combat with.

1.( ) officers   5.( ) not applicable
2.( ) non-commissioned officers
3.( ) warrant officers
4.( ) all three

132. He would probably distort reports to make himself
look better.

1.( ) officers   5.( ) not applicable
2.( ) non-commissioned officers
3.( ) warrant officers
4.( ) all three

133. He was overly ambitious at the expense of his
     subordinates and his unit.

     1.( ) officers   5.( ) not applicable
     2.( ) non-commissioned officers
     3.( ) warrant officers
     4.( ) all three

134. Tended to concentrate on the small unimportant
     things.

     1.( ) officers   5.( ) not applicable
     2.( ) non-commissioned officers
     3.( ) warrant officers
     4.( ) all three

135. Encouraged strong ties with the military unit.

     1.( ) officers   5.( ) not applicable
     2.( ) non-commissioned officers
     3.( ) warrant officers
     4.( ) all three

136. Used his position to take advantage of other soldiers.

     1.( ) officers   5.( ) not applicable
     2.( ) non-commissioned officers
     3.( ) warrant officers
     4.( ) all three

137. Stifled the initiative of others.

     1.( ) officers   5.( ) not applicable
     2.( ) non-commissioned officers
     3.( ) warrant officers
     4.( ) all three

138. He was willing to support his subordinates when they
     made mistakes.

     1 ( ) officers   5.( ) not applicable
     2.( ) non-commissioned officers
     3.( ) warrant officers
     4.( ) all three

139. Seemed more concerned about the troops than his
     own advancement.

     1.( ) officers   5.( ) not applicable
     2.( ) non-commissioned officers
     3.( ) warrant officers
     4.( ) all three

140. He would hesitate to take actions in the absence of instructions from his superiors.

    1.( ) officers   5.( ) not applicable
    2.( ) non-commissioned officers
    3.( ) warrant officers
    4.( ) all three

141. Tended to limit his contact with his men.

    1.( ) officers   5.( ) not applicable
    2.( ) non-commissioned officers
    3.( ) warrant officers
    4.( ) all three

142. He was generally available to his men to deal with their personal problems.

    1.( ) officers   5.( ) not applicable
    2.( ) non-commissioned officers
    3.( ) warrant officers
    4.( ) all three

143. He was a good example to young soldiers.

    1.( ) officers   5.( ) not applicable
    2.( ) non-commissioned officers
    3.( ) warrant officers
    4.( ) all three

144. Helped men overcome their lack of confidence.

    1.( ) officers   5.( ) not applicable
    2.( ) non-commissioned officers
    3.( ) warrant officers
    4.( ) all three

145. He was selfish.

    1.( ) officers   5.( ) not applicable
    2.( ) non-commissioned officers
    3.( ) warrant officers
    4.( ) all three

146. Tended to blame others for things he was supposed to do when they went wrong.

    1.( ) officers   5.( ) not applicable
    2.( ) non-commissioned officers
    3.( ) warrant officers
    4.( ) all three

147. Stuck to the letter of his superiors orders.

    1.( ) officers   5.( ) not applicable
    2.( ) non-commissioned officers
    3.( ) warrant officers
    4.( ) all three

148. About what percentage of non-commissioned officers that you knew in the military were conscript non-commissioned officers?

149. About what percentage of the non-commissioned officers that you knew in the military were professional, career-service non-commissioned officers?

150. In general, were conscript non-commissioned officers better than professional non-commissioned officers?

    1.( ) yes   2.( ) no   3.( ) both about the same

151. On a scale of from 1 to 10 in which 1 is the worst and 10 is the best, how well do you think your unit would do in actual combat?

    ‾1‾ ‾2‾ ‾3‾ ‾4‾ ‾5‾ ‾6‾ ‾7‾ ‾8‾ ‾9‾ ‾10‾
    WORST   BEST
                      (check one)

152. About how many hours a week are spent in political subjects and ideological indoctrination?

153. Among the soldiers that you knew, do you think that these kinds of classes are important in making a soldier want to be a good soldier?

    1.( ) yes   2.( ) no

154. On a scale of from 1 to 10 in which 1 is the least important and 10 is the most important, how important is a soldier's belief in Marxism-Leninism in motivating him to fight well?

    ‾1‾ ‾2‾ ‾3‾ ‾4‾ ‾5‾ ‾6‾ ‾7‾ ‾8‾ ‾9‾ ‾10‾
    LEAST IMPORTANT   MOST IMPORTANT

155. Did Soviet authorities make any effort to break up strong personal ties between soldiers?

1.( ) yes   2.( ) no

156. On a scale of from 1 to 10 in which 1 is the worst and 10 is the best, how would you rate the military training your unit received?

1	2	3	4	5	6	7	8	9	10
WORST									BEST

Codebook _____

COL #	Q #	CODE	ITEM	# CAT	CATEGORIES/ CODES
1-4	---	CANUN	Case number	---	
5-6	3	HOLONG	More than two	35	00-35
7-10	4	YERSER	Dates of ser	--	4000-7800
11	4	CATDAT	Serv Periods	6	1. Pre-war (PREWAR) 2. 1940-1952 (WAR) 3. 1953-1957 (POSTA) 4. 1958-1963 (CUBA) 5. 1964-1978 (MOD) 6. na (NA)
12	5	LIVAR	Living area	5	1. small village (VILL) 2. small town (TOWN) 3. large city (LCITY) 4. medium city (MCITY) 5. na (NA)
13	6	EDU	Education	7	1. less than 8 yrs (LESS) 2. incomplete secondary (INCSEC 3. complete secondary (COMSEC 4. technical degree (TECH) 5. some college (SOCOL) 6. complete college (COMCOL 7. na (NA)
14	6	EDUCAT	Ed. categories	4	1. Low (1-2) 2. Medium (3-4) 3. High (5-6) 4. na (NA)
15	7	MORED	Ed after serv.	3	1. yes 2. no 3. na
16	8	CIVSKL	Civilian skills	3	1. yes 2. no 3. na
17	9	BRANCH	Service branch	9	1. army (ARMY) 2. air force (AIR) 3. navy (NAVY) 4. strat. rocket forces (STRAT) 5. air defense (AIRDEF) 6. construction troops (CONSTR) 7. border guards (BORDER) 8. other (OTHER) 9. na (NA)

42

COL #	Q #	CODE	ITEM	# CAT	CATEGORIES/CODES
18	9	OTHER	Other branch	3	1. yes 2. no 3. na
19	10	RANK	Highest rank	5	1. private soldier (PRIV) 2. NCO (NCO) 3. warrant officer (WAR) 4. officer (OFF) 5. na (NA)
20	11	RANTI	Rank title	6	1. command enlisted (COMEN) 2. supervisory enlisted (SUPEN) 3. command officer (COMOFF) 4. supervisory officer (SUPOFF) 5. no command/supervisory (NONE) 6. na (NA)
21	12	UNTYP	Type of unit	8	1. infantry (INFANT) 2. tanks (TANKS) 3. artillery (ARTLY) 4. rockets (ROCKET) 5. support unit (SUPUN) 6. staff (STAFF) 7. other (OTHER) 8. na (NA)
22	12	OTHTYP	Other unit type		1. communications (COMM) 2. medical (MED) 3. chemical (CHEM) 4. political (POLIT) 5. ship (SHIP) 6. aircraft (AIR) 7. civil defense (CIVIL) 8. na (NA)
23	13	FRIEND	Close friends	3	1. yes 2. no 3. na
24	14	CLOFRI	# close friend	7	1. one (ONE) 2. two (TWO) 3. three (THREE) 4. four (FOUR) 5. five (FIVE) 6. six or more (SIX+) 7. none (NONE) 8. na (NA)

COL #	Q #	CODE	ITEM	# CAT	CATEGORIES/CODES
25	15	PLEEX	pleasant/un	3	1. pleasant (GOOD) 2. unpleasant (BAD) 3. na (NA)
26	16	AVOID	Avoid service	3	1. yes 2. no 3. na
27	17	FAMFEL	Family support	7	1. duty (DUTY) 2. good thing (GOOD) 3. not happy (NOHAP) 4. no feeling about it (NOFEL) 5. resigned (RESGD) 6. proud (PROUD) 7. na (NA)
28	18	FRIFEL	Friends support	4	1. good thing (GOOD) 2. proud of (PROUD) 3. not be avoided (NOOUT) 4. na (NA)
29	19	WASTE	Service as waste	3	1. yes 2. no 3. na
30	20	ANYGOD	Positive good	3	1. yes 2. no 3. na
31	21	MORDIF	Military difficult	3	1. yes 2. no 3. na
32	22	FRETIM	Free time	6	1. few hours (HOURS) 2. a day (DAY) 3. almost none (ALNONE) 4. every minute filled (EVMIN) 5. enough time (TIME) 6. na (NA)
33	23	PAY	Military/Civ pay	3	1. less (LESS) 2. more (MORE) 3. na (NA)
34	24	NUFPAY	Was pay enough	3	1. yes 2. no 3. na
35	25	FAMPAY	Family send money	3	1. yes 2. no 3. na

COL #	Q #	CODE	ITEM	# CAT	CATEGORIES/CODES
36	26	HOWAT	Hot water/ showers	3	1. yes 2. no 3. na
37	27	FOOD	Food Military/ Civ	4	1. better (BETTER) 2. worse (WORSE) 3. about the same (SAME) 4. na (NA)
38	28	QUALFD	Quality of food	3	1. yes 2. no 3. na
39	29	AMTFD	Amount of food	3	1. yes 2. no 3. na
40	30	QTRS	Living quarters	7	1. very good (VGOOD) 2. good (GOOD) 3. adequate (ADEQ) 4. poor (POOR) 5. bad (BAD) 6. very bad (VBAD) 7. na (NA)
41	31	HOUSE	Housing military/ civ	3	1. yes 2. no 3. na
42	32	OUTHSE	Toilets inside/ outside	3	1. inside (IN) 2. outside (OUT) 3. na (NA)
43	33	WARBAR	Warm barracks	3	1. yes 2. no 3. na
44	34	SORES	Sores from poor diet	3	1. yes 2. no 3. na
45	35	DIILL	Diet illness	3	1. yes 2. no 3. na
46	36	FDMOAN	Complaint/food	6	1. very much (MUCH) 2. often (OFTEN) 3. seldom (SELDOM) 4. rarely (RARELY) 5. almost never (ALNEV) 6. na (NA)

COL #	Q #	CODE	ITEM	# CAT	CATEGORIES/CODES	
47	37	OUTFOD	Get food outside	3	1. yes 2. no 3. na	
48	38	COMPRA	Common practice/ food	3	1. yes 2. no 3. na	
49	39	SELPRO	Selling state property	3	1. yes 2. no 3. na	
50	40	CROWD	Barracks over-crowded	3	1. yes 2. no 3. na	
51	41	USCRD	Usually crowded cond	3	1.yes 2. no 3. na	
52	42	NUMRM	Number in a room	9	1. two 2. three 3. four 4. five 5. six 6. seven 7. eight 8. more than eight 9. na	(TWO) (THREE) (FOUR) (FIVE) (SIX) (SEVEN) (EIGHT) (MORE) (NA)
53-56	43	SQMTRS	# Square meters/ room	--	0000-9999	
57	44	SPACE	Enough barracks space	3	1. yes 2. no 3. na	
58	45	PRICOM	Privacy com-plaints	3	1. yes 2. no 3. na	
59	46	PRIFIT	Fights/space-privacy	3	1. yes 2. no 3. na	
60	47	TRADE	Trade/sell to civ	3	1. yes 2. no 3. na	
61	48	SAVMNY	Save money in army	3	1. yes 2. no 3. na	

COL #	Q #	CODE	ITEM	# CAT	CATEGORIES/CODES
62	49	PAYCOM	Complaints about pay	6	1. very much (VYMCH) 2. often (OFTEN) 3. seldom (SELDOM) 4. rarely (RARELY) 5. almost never (ALNEV) 6. na (NA)
63	50	GIVEPA	Give pay to others	3	1. yes 2. no 3. na
64	51	OFPOST	# times allowed leave	5	1. one-two (1-2) 2. three-five (3-5) 3. six-ten (6-10) 4. over ten (+10) 5. na (NA)
65	52	EYE	Leave base alone	3	1. yes 2. no 3. na
66	53	HOEYE	How many times alone	6	1. never (NEVER) 2. one-two (1-2) 3. three-five (3-5) 4. six-ten (6-10) 5. over ten (+10) 6. na (NA)
67	54	GIRLS	Could you meet women	3	1. yes 2. no 3. na
68	55	METGIR	How often/girls	6	1. very often (VYOFT) 2. often (OFTEN) 3. seldom (SELDOM) 4. rarely (RARELY) 5. almost never (ALNEV) 6. na (NA)
69	56	GIROFF	Girls off post/ meet	3	1. yes 2. no 3. na
70	57	GIRPER	AWOL to meet girls	3	1. yes 2. no 3. na
71	58	GIRLV	# AWOL to meet girls	6	1. very often (VOFTEN) 2. often (OFTEN) 3. seldom (SELDOM) 4. rarely (RARELY) 5. almost never (ALNEV) 6. na (NA)

COL #	Q #	CODE	ITEM	# CAT	CATEGORIES/CODES
72	59	PUNGIR	Punishment AWOL/ girls	3	1. harsh (HARSH) 2. lenient (EASY) 3. na (NA)
73	60	ASOFF	Assault an officer	3	1. yes 2. no 3. na
74	61	ASNCO	Assault an NCO	3	1. yes 2. no 3. na
75	62	ASWAR	Assault a warrant officer	3	1. yes 2. no 3. na
76	63	ASTOR	Stories about assaults	3	1. yes 2. no 3. na
77	64	FIGHT	How good unit in combat	6	1. very well (VWELL) 2. fairly well (FAIR) 3. moderately well (MDTLY) 4. poorly (POOR) 5. very poorly (VPOOR) 6. na (NA)
78	65	MORALE	Officers care about morale	3	1. yes 2. no 3. na
79	66	DRINK	Drink more mil/ civ	3	1. military (MIL) 2. civilian (CIV) 3. na (NA)
80	67	OFDNK	Officer drinking habits	3	1. yes 2. no 3. na

NOTE: END FIRST CARD: BEGIN SECOND CARD

CHECK ALL ENTRIES FOR COLUMN # ACCURACY.

BEGIN SECOND CARD   BEGIN SECOND CARD

1-4	--	CASNUN	Casenumber	--	----------
5	68	DRUNK	Officer drunk	3	1. yes 2. no 3. na

48

COL #	Q #	CODE	ITEM	# CAT	CATEGORIES CODES
6	69	NCODNK	NCO drunk	3	1. yes 2. no 3. na
7	70	SOLDNK	Often soldier drunk	6	1. very often (VOFTEN) 2. often (OFTEN) 3. seldom (SELDOM) 4. rarely (RARELY) 5. almost never (ALNEV) 6. na (NA)
8	71	EXDNK	Excess drinking prob	7	1. yes 2. no 3. na
9	72	DNKPER	Drinking/unit perform	3	1. yes 2. no 3. na
10	73	PUNDNK	Punishment for drink	3	1. severe (SEVERE) 2. lenient (LENIENT) 3. na (NA)
11	74	ETHNIC	Unfair treatment	3	1. yes 2. no 3. na
12	75	COMETH	Unfair/ethnic/ common	3	1. yes 2. no 3. na
13	76	RECRU	Treat recruit unfair	6	1. very often (VOFTEN) 2. often (OFTEN) 3. seldom (SELDOM) 4. rarely (RARELY) 5. almost never (ALNEV) 6. na (NA)
14	77	NEGEF	Neg. effect on morale	3	1. yes 2. no 3. na
15	78	AWARE	Officer aware/ unfair	3	1. yes 2. no 3. na
16	79	SGTUN	Sgt. unfair treatment		1. very often (VYOFT) 2. often (OFTEN) 3. seldom (SELDOM) 4. rarely (RARELY) 5. almost never (ALNEV) 6. na (NA)

COL #	Q #	CODE	ITEM	# CAT	CATEGORIES/CODES
17	80	SUPGO	Go to superiors/ unfair	3	1. yes 2. no 3. na
18	81	TREAT	Civilian treat soldiers	3	1. yes 2. no 3. na
19	82	IDEOL	Ideology as motivator	5	1. most important (MOST) 2. very important (VERY) 3. not important (NOTIMP) 4. unimportant (UNIMP) 5. na (NA)
20	83	MOTIV	Factors motivating sold	6	1. comrade ties (TIES) 2. homefront (HOME) 3. officers care (CARE) 4. ideology (IDEO) 5. no coward (NOCOW) 6. na (NA)
21	84	KILL	Commit suicide	3	1. yes 2. no 3. na
22	85	ATKIL	Attempted suicide	3	1. yes 2. no 3. na
23	86	STORSU	Suicide stories/ units	3	1. yes 2. no 3. na
24	87	COMSTO	Suicide stories/ common	6	1. very common (VCOMM) 2. common (COMM) 3. uncommon (UNCOMM) 4. fairly rare (RARE) 5. almost never (ALNEV) 6. na (NA)
25	88	WHENSU	When suicide/ arrempts	3	1. first comes in (FIRST) 2. with unit (UNIT) 3. na (NA)
26	89	OFFSU	Officers suicide	3	1. yes 2. no 3. na
27	90	NCOSU	NCO suicide	3	1. yes 2. no 3. na

COL #	Q #	CODE	ITEM	# CAT	CATEGORIES/CODES
28	91	WARSU	Warrant officer suicide	3	1. yes 2. no 3. na
29	92	SUREL	Suicide for re-lease	3	1. yes 2. no 3. na
30	93	SUCARE	Superiors care/ suicide	3	1. yes 2. no 3. na
31	94	CONCO	# Conscript NCOs	9	1 - 8 9. na
32	95	PRONCO	# Professional NCOs	9	1 - 8 9. na
33	96	OFNUM	# of officers	9	1 - 8 9. na
34	97	WARNUM	# of warrant officers	9	1 - 8 9. na
35	98	OFQUAL	Officer quality	7	1. extremely good (EXGOOD) 2. good (GOOD) 3. average (AVG) 4. fair (FAIR) 5. poor (POOR) 6. very poor (VPOOR) 7. na (NA)
36	99	NCOQUAL	NCO quality	7	1. extremely good (EXGOOD) 2. good (GOOD) 3. average (AVER) 4. fair (FAIR) 5. poor (POOR) 6. very poor (VYPOR) 7. na (NA)
37	100	CLOFEL	Close with com-rades	6	1. very close (VCLOSE) 2. close (CLOSE) 3. moderately close (MCLOSE) 4. not close (NCLOSE) 5. few bonds (FEW) 6. na (NA)

COL #	Q #	CODE	ITEM	# CAT	CATEGORIES/CODES
38	101	PRIDE	Pride in military unit	7	1. very strongly (VYSTR) 2. strongly (STRNG) 3. moderately (MDTY) 4. not very strong (NOSTG) 5. not concern me (NOCON) 6. no pride (NOPRD) 7. na (NA)
39	102	DSRT	Desertion	3	1. yes 2. no 3. na
40	103	OFFDRT	Officer desertion	3	1. yes 2. no 3. na
41	104	WARDRT	Warrant officer desertion	3	1. yes 2. no 3. na
42	105	NCODRT	NCO desertion	3	1. yes 2. no 3. na
43	106	DRTCOM	Commoness of desertion	6	1. very common (VCOMM) 2. common (COMM) 3. generally uncommon (GUNCOM) 4. rare (RARE) 5. almost never (ALNEV) 6. na (NA)
44	107	AWOL	Awol rate	7	1. quite often (QOFT) 2. often (OFTEN) 3. fairly often (FAOFT) 4. not very much (NOMCH) 5. rarely (RARE) 6. almost never (ALNEV) 7. na (NA)
45	108	WOLREA	Reasons for Awol	9	1. get vodka (VODKA) 2. meet women (WOMEN) 3. escape mil life (ESCLIF) 4. escape for good (ESCGD) 5. family problems (FAMILY) 6. unfair treatment (TREAT) 7. extra food (FOOD) 8. drugs (DRUGS) 9. na (NA)

COL #	Q #	CODE	ITEM	# CAT	CATEGORIES/CODES
46	108	WOLREB	Reasons for Awol (2)	9	1. get vodka (VODKA) 2. meet women (WOMEN) 3. escape short time (ESLIF) 4. escape for good (ESGD) 5. family problems (FAM) 6. unfair treatment (TREAT) 7. extra food (FOOD) 8. drugs (DRUGS) 9. na (NA)
47	108	WOLREC	Reason for Awol (3)	9	1. get vodka (VODKA) 2. meet women (WOMEN) 3. escape short time (ESLIF) 4. escape for good (ESGD) 5. family problems (FAM) 6. unfair treatment (TREAT) 7. extra food (FOOD) 8. drugs (DRUGS) 9. na (NA)
48	109	WOLCO	Superiors concern/ Awol	3	1. yes 2. no 3. na
49	110	SUPDRT	Superiors concern/ desertion	3	1. yes 2. no 3. na
50	111	PROBA	Awol a big problem		1. yes 2. no 3. na
51	112	PROBD	Desertion a big problem	3	1. yes 2. no 3. na
52	113	AWOLP	Punishment for Awol	3	1. harsh (HARSH) 2. lenient (EASY) 3. na (NA)
53	114	INPER	Interested/per- sonal Problem	5	1. officer (OFF) 2. NCO (NCO) 3. warramt (WAR) 4. all three (ALL) 5. na (NA)
54	115	SHOINT	Shows interest in men	5	1. officer (OFF) 2. NCO (NCO) 3. warrant (WAR) 4. all three (ALL) 5. na (NA)

COL #	Q #	CODE	ITEM	# CAT	CATEGORIES/CODES
55	116	CARADV	Career advancement	5	1. officer (OFF) 2. NCO (NCO) 3. warrant (WAR) 4. all three (ALL) 5. na (NA)
56	117	COGS	Treated men impersonally	5	1. officer (OFF) 2. NCO (NCO) 3. warrant (WAR) 4. all three (ALL) 5. na (NA)
57	118	STODUP	Stood up for his men	5	1 officer (OFF) 2. NCO (NCO) 3. warrant (WAR) 4. all three (ALL) 5. na (NA)
58	119	CRISUB	Criticised subordinates	5	1. officer (OFF) 2. NCO (NCO) 3. warrant (WAR) 4. all three (ALL) 5. na (NA)
59	120	HARSHP	Shared hardship with men	5	1. officer (OFF) 2. NCO (NCO) 3. warrant (WAR) 4. all three (ALL) 5. na (NA)
60	121	HADTHI	Men got what needed	5	1. officer (OFF) 2. NCO (NCO) 3. warrant (WAR) 4. all three (ALL) 5. na (NA)
61	122	EXAMP	Set example for men	5	1. officer (OFF) 2. NCO (NCO) 3. warrant (WAR) 4. all three (ALL) 5. na (NA)
62	123	DIST	Was too distant	5	1. officer (OFF) 2. NCO (NCO) 3. warrant (WAR) 4. all three (ALL) 5. na (NA)

COL #	Q #	CODE	ITEM	# CAT	CATEGORIES/CODES	
63	124	JUDGE	Had judgement/ combat	5	1. officer	(OFF)
					2. NCO	(NCO)
					3. warrant	(WAR)
					4. all three	(ALL)
					5. na	(NA)
64	125	KNEWRE	Knew men/ respect cap	5	1. officer	(OFF)
					2. NCO	(NCO)
					3. warrant	(WAR)
					4. all three	(ALL)
					5. na	(NA)
65	126	NOPETI	No personal ties	5	1. officer	(OFF)
					2. NCO	(NCO)
					3. warrant	(WAR)
					4. all three	(ALL)
					5. na	(NA)
66	127	MORHI	Made morale high	5	1. officer	(OFF)
					2. NCO	(NCO)
					3. warrant	(WAR)
					4. all three	(ALL)
					5. na	(NA)
67	128	WRONG	Avoided respon- sibility	5	1. officer	(OFF)
					2. NCO	(NCO)
					3. warrant	(WAR)
					4. all three	(ALL)
					5. na	(NA)
68	129	SYMLIS	Listened to prob- lems	5	1. officer	(OFF)
					2. NCO	(NCO)
					3. warrant	(WAR)
					4. all three	(ALL)
					5. na	(NA)
69	130	PRAISE	Praised troops/ good job	5	1. officer	(OFF)
					2. NCO	(NCO)
					3. warrant	(WAR)
					4. all three	(ALL)
					5. na	(NA)
70	131	COMGUD	Good man in combat	5	1. officer	(OFF)
					2. NCO	(NCO)
					3. warrant	(WAR)
					4. all three	(ALL)
					5. na	(NA)
71	132	DISTO	Distort reports/ career	5	1. officer	(OFF)
					2. NCO	(NCO)
					3. warrant	(WAR)
					4. all three	(ALL)
					5. na	(NA)

COL #	Q #	CODE	ITEM	# CAT	CATEGORIES/CODES	
72	133	OVAMB	Overly ambitious	5	1. officer	(OFF)
					2. NCO	(NCO)
					3. warrant	(WAR)
					4. all three	(ALL)
					5. na	(NA)
73	134	UNIMP	Looks at small things	5	1. officer	(OFF)
					2. NCO	(NCO)
					3. warrant	(WAR)
					4. all three	(ALL)
					5. na	(NA)
74	135	UTIES	Made strong unit ties	5	1. officer	(OFF)
					2. NCO	(NCO)
					3. warrant	(WAR)
					4. all three	(ALL)
					5. na	(NA)
75	136	USEPO	Used position/ take advantage	5	1. officer	(OFF)
					2. NCO	(NCO)
					3. warrant	(WAR)
					4. all three	(ALL)
					5. na	(NA)
76	137	STIFLE	Stifled initiative	5	1. officer	(OFF)
					2. NCO	(NCO)
					3. warrant	(WAR)
					4. all three	(ALL)
					5. na	(NA)
77	138	MISTKE	Support men when mistakes	5	1. officer	(OFF)
					2. NCO	(NCO)
					3. warrant	(WAR)
					4. all three	(ALL)
					5. na	(NA)
78	139	TRPCON	Concerned about troops more	5	1. officer	(OFF)
					2. NCO	(NCO)
					3. warrant	(WAR)
					4. all three	(ALL)
					5. na	(NA)
79	140	HESIT	Hesitate to act	5	1. officer	(OFF)
					2. NCO	(NCO)
					3. warrant	(WAR)
					4. all three	(ALL)
					5. na	(NA)
80	141	LIMCON	Limit contact with men	5	1. officer	(OFF)
					2. NCO	(NCO)
					3. warrant	(WAR)
					4. all three	(ALL)
					5. na	(NA)

COL #	Q #	CODE	ITEM	# CAT	CATEGORIES/CODES	
1 - 4	--	CASNUN	Case number	--	------	
5	142	PPROB	Available/personal prob	5	1. officer 2. NCO 3. warrant 4. all three 5. na	(OFF) (NCO) (WAR) (ALL) (NA)
6	143	GOODEX	Good example for men	5	1. officer 2. NCO 3. warrant 4. all three 5. na	(OFF) (NCO) (WAR) (ALL) (NA)
7	144	LACKCO	Overcome lack confidence	5	1. officer 2. NCO 3. warrant 4. all three 5. na	(OFF) (NCO) (WAR) (ALL) (NA)
8	145	SELF	Selfish person	5	1. officer 2. NCO 3. warrant 4. all three 5. na	(OFF) (NCO) (WAR) (ALL) (NA)
9	146	BLAME	Blame others for errors	5	1. officer 2. NCO 3. warrant 4. all three 5. na	(OFF) (NCO) (WAR) (ALL) (NA)
10	147	STUCK	Stuck to letter orders	5	1. officer 2. NCO 3. warrant 4. all three 5. na	(OFF) (NCO) (WAR) (ALL) (NA)
11-12	148	PERCON	% conscript NCO	99	00 - 99	
13-14	149	PERPRO	% professional NCO	99	00 - 99	
15	150	WHOBET	Who was better	3	1. yes 2. no 3. na	

COL #	Q #	CODE	ITEM	# CAT	CATEGORIES/CODES
16-17	151	SCALCO	Scale of combat ability	10	00 - 10
18-19	152	INDOC	Hours a week/ indoctrin	99	00 - 99
20	153	CLASS	Are indoc classes good	3	1. yes 2. no 3. na
21-22	154	MARX	Marxism as motivator	10	00 - 09
23	155	BRKFRI	Break up friendships	3	1. yes 2. no 3. na
24-25	156	TRAIN	Quality of training	10	00 - 99

FINISH FINISH FINISH FINISH

List
of
Tables _____

Table

Table

Table

Data
Tables _____

Table 1

4: When were you in the military service? (CATDAT)

```
1. Pre-war        (PREWAR)
2. 1940-1952      (WAR)
3. 1953-1957      (POSTA)
4. 1958-1963      (CUBA)
5. 1964-1978      (MOD)
6. Not applicable(NA)
```

CATDAT = Serv periods

RANGE	FREQ	%	SG
1	5	4.4	PREWAR
2	24	21.2	WAR
3	21	18.6	POSTA
4	13	11.5	CUBA
5	50	44.2	MOD
6	0	0.0	xNA

Table 2

5: What type of living area did you come from before you entered the military? (LIVAR)

```
1. Small rural village (VILL)
2. Small urban town    (TOWN)
3. Large city          (LCITY)
4. Medium size city    (MCITY)
5. Not applicable      (NA)
```

LIVAR = Living area

RANGE	FREQ	%	SG
1	4	3.5	VILL
2	4	3.5	TOWN
3	81	71.7	LCITY
4	24	21.2	MCITY
5	0	0.0	xNA

Table 3

\# 6: What was the highest level of education you achieved
before you went into the military? (EDU)

1. Less than 8 years   (LESS)
2. Incomplete secondary (INCSEC)
3. Complete secondary   (COMSEC)
4. Technical degree   (TECH)
5. Some college   (SOCOL)
6. Complete college   (COMCOL)
7. Not applicable   (NA)

EDU = Education

RANGE	FREQ	%	SG
1	12	10.6	LESS
2	12	10.6	INCSEC
3	33	29.2	COMSEC
4	26	23.0	TECH
5	13	11.5	SOMCOL
6	13	11.5	COMCOL
7	4	3.5	xNA

Table 4

\# 6: What was the highest level of education you achieved
before you went into the military? (EDUCAT)

1. Low   (1-2)
2. Medium   (3-4)
3. High   (5-6)
4. Not applicable (NA)

EDUCAT = Ed. categories

RANGE	FREQ	%	SG
1	24	21.2	LOW
2	59	52.2	MEDIUM
3	26	23.0	HIGH
4	4	3.5	xNA

Table 5

7: Did you obtain more education after you left military
service? (MORED)

1. Yes   (YES)
2. No   (NO)
3. Not applicable (NA)

MORED = Ed after serv.

RANGE	FREQ	%	SG
1	65	57. 5	YES
2	48	42. 5	NO
3	0	0. 0	xMISSING

Table 6

8: Did you learn any useful civilian skills while you
were in the military? (CIVSKL)

1. Yes   (YES)
2. No   (NO)
3. Not applicable (NA)

CIVSKL = Civilian skills

RANGE	FREQ	%	SG
1	32	28. 3	YES
2	81	71. 7	NO
3	0	0. 0	xMISSING

Table 7

9: What part of the military were you in? (BRANCH)

    1. Army   (ARMY)
    2. Air force   (AIR)
    3. Navy   (NAVY)
    4. Strategic rocket forces   (STRAT)
    5. Air defense corps   (AIRDEF)
    6. Construction troops   (CONSTR)
    7. Border guards   (BORDER)
    8. Other   (OTHER)
    9. Not applicable   (NA)

BRANCH = Service branch

RANGE	FREQ	%	SG
1	66	58.4	ARMY
2	0	0.0	AIR
3	1	0.9	NAVY
4	6	5.3	STRAT
5	17	15.0	AIRDEF
6	20	17.7	CONSTR
7	2	1.8	BORDER
8	1	0.9	OTHER
9	0	0.0	xNA

Table 8

9: What part of the military were you in? (OTHER)

    1. Yes   (YES)
    2. No   (NO)
    3. Not applicable   (NA)

OTHER = Other branch

RANGE	FREQ	%	SG
1	2	1.8	YES
2	2	1.8	NO
3	109	96.5	xMISSING

Table 9

10: What was the highest rank you attained? (RANK)

```
            1. Private soldier           (PRIV)
            2. Non-commissioned officer  (NCO)
            3. Warrant officer           (WAR)
            4. Officer                   (OFF)
            5. Not applicable            (NA)
```

RANK = Highest rank

RANGE	FREQ	%	SG
1	59	52.2	PRIV
2	30	26.5	NCO
3	3	2.7	WAR
4	20	17.7	OFF
5	1	0.9	xNA

Table 10

11: What was your actual rank title? (RANTI)

```
            1. Command enlisted          (COMEN)
            2. Supervisory enlisted      (SUPEN)
            3. Command officer           (COMOFF)
            4. Supervisory officer       (SUPOFF)
            5. No command/supervisory    (NONE)
            6. Not applicable            (NA)
```

RANTI = Rank title

RANGE	FREQ	%	SG
1	18	15.9	COMEN
2	16	14.2	SUPEN
3	12	10.6	COMOFF
4	9	8.0	SUPOFF
5	57	50.4	NONE
6	1	0.9	xNA

Table 11

12: What type of military unit were you in? (UNTYP)

```
              1. Infantry            (INFANT)
              2. Tanks               (TANKS)
              3. Artillery           (ARTLY)
              4. Rockets             (ROCKET)
              5. Rear support unit   (SUPUN)
              6. Staff unit          (STAFF)
              7. Other               (OTHER)
              8. Not applicable      (NA)
```

UNTYP = type of unit

RANGE	FREQ	%	SG
1	29	25. 7	INFANT
2	13	11. 5	TANKS
3	11	9. 7	ARTLY
4	23	20. 4	ROCKET
5	30	26. 5	SUPUN
6	4	3. 5	STAFF
7	3	2. 7	OTHER
8	0	0. 0	xNA

Table 12

12: What type of military unit were you in? (OTHTYP)

```
              1. Communications  (COMM)
              2. Medical         (MED)
              3. Chemical        (CHEM)
              4. Political       (POLIT)
              5. Ship            (SHIP)
              6. Aircraft        (AIR)
              7. Civil defense   (CIVIL)
              8. Not applicable  (NA)
```

OTHTYP = Other unit type

RANGE	FREQ	%	SG
1	2	1. 8	COMM
2	1	0. 9	MEDIC
3	0	0. 0	CHEM
4	2	1. 8	POLIT
5	1	0. 9	SHIP
6	0	0. 0	AIR
7	1	0. 9	CIVIL
8	106	93. 8	xNA

Table 13

13: Did you make any close friends while you were in the military? (FRIEND)

    1. Yes   (YES)
    2. No   (NO)
    3. Not applicable (NA)

FRIEND = Close friends

RANGE	FREQ	%	SG
1	78	69.0	YES
2	35	31.0	NO
3	0	0.0	xMISSING

Table 14

14: About how many close friends did you have in the military? (CLOFRI)

    1. One   (ONE)
    2. Two   (TWO)
    3. Three   (THREE)
    4. Four   (FOUR)
    5. Five   (FIVE)
    6. Six or more   (SIX+)
    7. None   (NONE)
    8. Not applicable (NA)

CLOFRI = # close friend

RANGE	FREQ	%	SG
1	10	8.8	ONE
2	25	22.1	TWO
3	21	18.6	THREE
4	5	4.4	FOUR
5	3	2.7	FIVE
6	15	13.3	SIX+
7	34	30.1	NONE
8	0	0.0	xNA

Table 15

15: In general was your service in the military a pleasant
       or unpleasant experience? (PLEEX)

```
        1. Pleasant        (GOOD)
        2. Unpleasant      (BAD)
        3. Not applicable  (NA)
```

```
PLEEX = Pleasant/un

RANGE   FREQ     %     SG
=================================
   1      18    15.9   GOOD
   2      91    80.5   BAD
   3       4     3.5  xNA
```

Table 16

16: If you could have avoided going into the military
       like some people did, would you have avoided it?
                              (AVOID)

```
        1. Yes             (YES)
        2. No              (NO)
        3. Not applicable  (NA)
```

```
AVOID = Avoid service

RANGE   FREQ     %     SG
=================================
   1      78    69.0   YES
   2      33    29.2   NO
   3       2     1.8  xMISSING
```

Table 17

17: How did your family feel about your going into the
military? (FAMFEL)

```
1. Thought it was my duty                      (DUTY)
2. Thought it was a good thing                 (GOOD)
3. Were generally not happy with my going      (NOHAP)
4. Had no real feeling about it                (NOFEL)
5. Resigned because it could not be avoided    (RESGD)
6. Were proud that I was serving my country    (PROUD)
7. Not applicable                              (NA)
```

FAMFEL = Family support

RANGE	FREQ	%	SG
1	7	6.2	DUTY
2	6	5.3	GOOD
3	7	6.2	NOHAP
4	2	1.8	NOFEL
5	86	76.1	RESGD
6	1	0.9	PROUD
7	4	3.5	xNA

Table 18

18: Did your friends think that going into the military
was a good thing, something to be proud of, or
something that could not be avoided? (FRIFEL)

```
1. A good thing                              (GOOD)
2. Something to be proud of                  (PROUD)
3. Something that could not be avoided       (NOOUT)
4. Not applicable                            (NA)
```

FRIFEL = Friends support

RANGE	FREQ	%	SG
1	5	4.4	GOOD
2	6	5.3	PROUD
3	100	88.5	NOOUT
4	2	1.8	xNA

Table 19

19: At the time you were in the military did you think
it was a waste of time? (WASTE)

1. Yes   (YES)
2. No   (NO)
3. Not applicable (NA)

WASTE = Service as waste

RANGE	FREQ	%	SG
1	94	83.2	YES
2	16	14.2	NO
3	3	2.7	xMISSING

Table 20

20: Do you think you got anything good out of going in
the military? (ANYGOD)

1. Yes   (YES)
2. No   (NO)
3. Not applicable (NA)

ANYGOD = Positive good

RANGE	FREQ	%	SG
1	31	27.4	YES
2	78	69.0	NO
3	4	3.5	xMISSING

Table 21

21: Was the military life more difficult than you expected?
(MORDIF)

    1. Yes   (YES)
    2. No   (NO)
    3. Not applicable (NA)

MORDIF = Military difficult

RANGE	FREQ	%	SG
1	65	57.5	YES
2	46	40.7	NO
3	2	1.8	xMISSING

Table 22

22: About how much free time did you have to yourself
in an average week? (FRETIM)

    1. Only a few hours   (HOURS)
    2. About a day   (DAY)
    3. Almost none at all   (ALNONE)
    4. Every minute was accounted for (EVMIN)
    5. Generally enough free time   (TIME)
    6. Not applicable   (NA)

FRETIM = Free time

RANGE	FREQ	%	SG
1	36	31.9	HOURS
2	27	23.9	DAY
3	20	17.7	ALNONE
4	7	6.2	EVMIN
5	22	19.5	TIME
6	1	0.9	xNA

Table 23

23: Compared to what you were being payed before you went into the military, was military pay more or less? (PAY)

      1. Less   (LESS)
      2. More   (MORE)
      3. Not applicable (NA)

PAY = Military/Civ pay

RANGE	FREQ	%	SG
1	89	78.8	LESS
2	18	15.9	MORE
3	6	5.3	xNA

Table 24

24: Was your pay enough for your needs? (NUFPAY)

      1. Yes   (YES)
      2. No   (NO)
      3. Not applicable (NA)

NUFPAY = Was pay enough

RANGE	FREQ	%	SG
1	24	21.2	YES
2	87	77.0	NO
3	2	1.8	xMISSING

Table 25

25: Did your family ever have to send you money so that
you could get by? (FAMPAY)

1. Yes   (YES)
2. No   (NO)
3. Not applicable (NA)

FAMPAY = Family send money

RANGE	FREQ	%	SG
1	69	61. 1	YES
2	43	38. 1	NO
3	1	0. 9	xMISSING

Table 26

26: Was hot water available every day for showers in
your military unit? (HOWAT)

1. Yes   (YES)
2. No   (NO)
3. Not applicable (NA)

HOWAT = Hot water/showers

RANGE	FREQ	%	SG
1	5	4. 4	YES
2	108	95. 6	NO
3	0	0. 0	xMISSING

88

Table 27

27: Was the food in the military generally better or
      worse than in civilian life? (FOOD)

        1. Better   (BETTER)
        2. Worse   (WORSE)
        3. About the same (SAME)
        4. Not applicable (NA)

_____

FOOD = Food Military/Civ

    RANGE   FREQ   %   SG
    =================================
      1   6   5.3   BETTER
      2   96   85.0   WORSE
      3   11   9.7   SAME
      4   0   0.0   xNA

Table 28

28: Was the quality of food you received adequate? (QUALFD)

        1. Yes   (YES)
        2. No   (NO)
        3. Not applicable (NA)

_____

QUALFD = Quality of food

    RANGE   FREQ   %   SG
    =================================
      1   29   25.7   YES
      2   83   73.5   NO
      3   1   0.9   xMISSING

Table 29

29: Was the amount of food you received adequate for
your needs? (AMTFD)

        1. Yes   (YES)
        2. No   (NO)
        3. Not applicable (NA)

AMTFD = Amount of food

RANGE	FREQ	%	SG
1	59	52. 2	YES
2	54	47. 8	NO
3	0	0. 0	xMISSING

Table 30

30: In general, how would you describe the living quarter
you lived in while in the military? (QTRS)

        1. Very good (VGOOD)
        2. Good   (GOOD)
        3. Adequate (ADEQ)
        4. Poor   (POOR)
        5. Bad   (BAD)
        6. Very bad   (VBAD)
        7. Not applicable (NA)

QTRS = Living quarters

RANGE	FREQ	%	SG
2	2	1. 8	GOOD
3	42	37. 2	ADEQ
4	21	18. 6	POOR
5	23	20. 4	BAD
6	25	22. 1	VBAD
7	0	0. 0	xNA

Table 31

31: In your experience was housing in the military
generally better than what you were used to in
civilian life? (HOUSE)

1. Yes   (YES)
2. No   (NO)
3. Not applicable (NA)

HOUSE = Housing military/civ

RANGE	FREQ	%	SG
1	10	8.8	YES
2	103	91.2	NO
3	0	0.0	xMISSING

Table 32

32: Were the toilets located inside the barracks or
was it necessary to go outside? (OUTHSE)

1. Inside   (IN)
2. Outside   (OUT)
3. Not applicable (NA)

OUTHSE = Toilets inside/outside

RANGE	FREQ	%	SG
1	38	33.6	IN
2	73	64.6	OUT
3	2	1.8	xNA

Table 33

33: Were the barracks normally warm enough in winter to keep you comfortable? (WARBAR)

1. Yes   (YES)
2. No   (NO)
3. Not applicable (NA)

WARBAR = Warm barracks

RANGE	FREQ	%	SG
=======	======	======	==========
1	63	55.8	YES
2	47	41.6	NO
3	3	2.7	xMISSING

Table 34

34: Did anyone in your unit ever develop sores or carbuncles from having a poor diet? (SORES)

1. Yes   (YES)
2. No   (NO)
3. Not applicable (NA)

SORES = Sores from poor diet

RANGE	FREQ	%	SG
=======	======	======	==========
1	71	62.8	YES
2	33	29.2	NO
3	9	8.0	xMISSING

Table 35

35: Did anyone in your unit ever develop any other
illness because of improper or inadequate diet?
(DIILL)

  1. Yes   (YES)
  2. No   (NO)
  3. Not applicable (NA)

DIILL = Diet illness

RANGE	FREQ	%	SG
1	74	65.5	YES
2	26	23.0	NO
3	13	11.5	xMISSING

Table 36

36: How much did the troops complain about the food?
(FDMOAN)

  1. Very much   (VMUCH)
  2. Often   (OFTEN)
  3. Seldom   (SELDOM)
  4. Rarely   (RARELY)
  5. Almost never (ALNEV)
  6. Not applicable (NA)

FDMOAN = Complaint/food

RANGE	FREQ	%	SG
1	17	15.0	VMUCH
2	37	32.7	OFTEN
3	29	25.7	SELDOM
4	15	13.3	RARELY
5	13	11.5	ALNEV
6	2	1.8	xNA

Table 37

37: Did you or anyone in your unit ever obtain extra
food from sources outside the military? (OUTFOD)

       1. Yes   (YES)
       2. No   (NO)
       3. Not applicable (NA)

OUTFOD = Get food outside

RANGE	FREQ	%	SG
1	83	73.5	YES
2	28	24.8	NO
3	2	1.8	xMISSING

Table 38

38: Was this a common practice? (COMPRA)

       1. Yes   (YES)
       2. No   (NO)
       3. Not applicable (NA)

COMPRA = Common practice/food

RANGE	FREQ	%	SG
1	57	50.4	YES
2	54	47.8	NO
3	2	1.8	xMISSING

Table 39

39: Did you ever hear of anyone in your unit selling
state property to get some extra money? (SELPRO)

        1. Yes   (YES)
        2. No   (NO)
        3. Not applicable(NA)

SELPRO = Selling state property

RANGE	FREQ	%	SG
1	78	69.0	YES
2	33	29.2	NO
3	2	1.8	xMISSING

Table 40

40: Were the troop barracks usually overcrowded? (CROWD)

        1. Yes   (YES)
        2. No   (NO)
        3. Not applicable (NA)

CROWD = Barracks overcrowded

RANGE	FREQ	%	SG
1	71	62.8	YES
2	39	34.5	NO
3	3	2.7	xMISSING

Table 41

41: Was this the usual condition in most units that you
know of? (USCRD)

1. Yes   (YES)
2. No   (NO)
3. Not applicable (NA)

USCRD = Usually crowded cond

RANGE	FREQ	%	SG
1	70	61.9	YES
2	29	25.7	NO
3	14	12.4	xMISSING

Table 42

44: Did you have enough space and privacy in your
barracks? (SPACE)

1. Yes   (YES)
2. No   (NO)
3. Not applicable (NA)

SPACE = Enough barracks space

RANGE	FREQ	%	SG
1	10	8.8	YES
2	99	87.6	NO
3	4	3.5	xMISSING

Table 43

45 : Is the lack of space and privacy a major complaint
          among the soldiers? (PRICOM)

        1. Yes   (YES)
        2. No   (NO)
        3. Not applicable (NA)

_____

PRICOM = Privacy complaints

RANGE FREQ   %   SG
==================================
   1   54   47. 8   YES
   2   51   45. 1   NO
   3   8   7. 1   xMISSING

Table 44

46 : Does this lack of space or privacy lead to frequent
          fights among the soldiers? (PRIFIT)

        1. Yes   (YES)
        2. No   (NO)
        3. Not applicable (NA)

_____

PRIFIT = Fights/space-privacy

RANGE FREQ   %   SG
==================================
   1   31   27. 4   YES
   2   75   66. 4   NO
   3   7   6. 2   xMISSING

Table 45

\# 47: Could you make some extra money in the military by trading or selling things to other soldiers or to civilians? (TRADE)

1. Yes   (YES)
2. No   (NO)
3. Not applicable (NA)

TRADE = Trade/sell To civ

RANGE	FREQ	%	SG
1	18	15.9	YES
2	90	79.6	NO
3	5	4.4	xMISSING

Table 46

\# 48: While you were in the military were you able to save some money for when you returned to civilian life? (SAVMNY)

1. Yes   (YES)
2. No   (NO)
3. Not applicable (NA)

SAVMNY = Save money in army

RANGE	FREQ	%	SG
1	16	14.2	YES
2	95	84.1	NO
3	2	1.8	xMISSING

Table 47

49: In general how much did the troops complain about
the pay they received? (PAYCOM)

        1. Very much   (VYMCH)
        2. Often   (OFTEN)
        3. Seldom   (SELDOM)
        4. Rarely   (RARELY)
        5. Almost never (ALNEV)
        6. Not applicable (NA)

PAYCOM = Complaints about pay

RANGE	FREQ	%	SG
1	18	15.9	VMUCH
2	25	22.1	OFTEN
3	19	16.8	SELDOM
4	10	8.8	RARELY
5	40	35.4	ALNEV
6	1	0.9	xNA

Table 48

50: Did you ever hear stories about soldiers who were
forced to give some of their pay to other soldiers
or to non-commissioned officers? (GIVEPA)

        1. Yes   (YES)
        2. No   (NO)
        3. Not applicable (NA)

GIVEPA = Give pay to others

RANGE	FREQ	%	SG
1	34	30.1	YES
2	76	67.3	NO
3	3	2.7	xMISSING

Table 49

51: In the whole time you were in the military, how
many times were you allowed to leave the base for
your own recreation? (OFPOST)

      1. One-two   (1-2)
      2. Three-five   (3-5)
      3. Six-ten   (6-10)
      4. Over ten   (+10)
      5. Not applicable (NA)

OFPOST = # times allowed leave

RANGE	FREQ	%	SG
1	22	19.5	1-2
2	10	8.8	3-5
3	4	3.5	6-10
4	61	54.0	+10
5	16	14.2	xNA

Table 50

52: Were you ever allowed to leave the base without
the company of some higher ranking soldier to keep
an eye on things? (EYE)

      3. Yes   (YES)
      2. No   (NO)
      3. Not applicable (NA)

EYE = Leave base alone

RANGE	FREQ	%	SG
1	82	72.6	YES
2	26	23.0	NO
3	5	4.4	xMISSING

Table 51

53: How many times? (HOEYE)

1. Never   (NEVER)
2. One-two   (1-2)
3. Three - five   (3-5)
4. Six - ten   (6-10)
5. Over ten   (+10)
6. Not applicable   (NA)

HOEYE = How many times alone

RANGE	FREQ	%	SG
1	18	15.9	NEVER
2	11	9.7	1-2
3	9	8.0	3-5
4	4	3.5	6-10
5	54	47.8	+10
6	17	15.0	xNA

Table 52

54: During your time in the military were you able to
        meet women? (GIRLS)

1. Yes   (YES)
2. No   (NO)
3. Not applicable   (NA)

GIRLS = Could you meet women

RANGE	FREQ	%	SG
1	71	62.8	YES
2	40	35.4	NO
3	2	1.8	xMISSING

Table 53

55: How often did you get to meet women? (METGIR)

       1. Very often   (VYOFT)
       2. Often   (OFTEN)
       3. Seldom   (SELDOM)
       4. Rarely   (RARELY)
       5. Almost never   (ALNEV)
       6. Not applicable (NA)

METGIR = How often/girls

RANGE	FREG	%	SG
1	6	5.3	VOFTEN
2	10	8.8	OFTEN
3	25	22.1	SELDOM
4	29	25.7	RARELY
5	33	29.2	ALNEV
6	10	8.8	xNA

Table 54

56: Could you visit these women in places off the
military base? (GIROFF)

       1. Yes   (YES)
       2. No   (NO)
       3. Not applicable (NA)

GIROFF = Girls off post/meet

RANGE	FREG	%	SG
1	68	60.2	YES
2	39	34.5	NO
3	6	5.3	xMISSING

Table 55

\# 57: Did soldiers have to leave the base without permission to see women? (GIRPER)

      1. Yes   (YES)
      2. No   (NO)
      3. Not applicable (NA)

GIRPER = AWOL to meet girls

RANGE	FREQ	%	SG
1	84	74.3	YES
2	27	23.9	NO
3	2	1.8	xMISSING

Table 56

\# 58: How often did soldiers in your unit leave the base
without permission to see women? (GIRLV)

      1. Very often   (VOFTEN)
      2. Often   (OFTEN)
      3. Seldom   (SELDOM)
      4. Rarely   (RARELY)
      5. Almost never (ALNEV)
      6. Not applicable (NA)

GIRLV = \# AWOL to meet girls

RANGE	FREQ	%	SG
1	18	15.9	VOFTEN
2	34	30.1	OFTEN
3	28	24.8	SELDOM
4	18	15.9	RARELY
5	12	10.6	ALNEV
6	3	2.7	xNA

Table 57

59: If you were caught leaving the base without per-
mission to visit a woman was the punishment
generally harsh or lenient? (PUNGIR)

      1. Harsh   (HARSH)
      2. Lenient   (EASY)
      3. Not applicable (NA)

PUNGIR = Punishment AWOL/girls

RANGE	FREQ	%	SG
1	91	80.5	HARSH
2	11	9.7	EASY
3	11	9.7	xNA

Table 58

60: Did anyone in your unit ever physically assault
an officer? (ASOFF)

      1. Yes   (YES)
      2. No   (NO)
      3. Not applicable (NA)

ASOFF = Assault an officer

RANGE	FREQ	%	SG
1	41	36.3	YES
2	69	61.1	NO
3	3	2.7	xMISSING

Table 59

61: Did anyone in your unit ever physically assault
an non-commissioned officer? (ASNCO)

1. Yes   (YES)
2. No   (NO)
3. Not applicable (NA)

ASNCO = Assault an NCO

RANGE	FREQ	%	SG
1	71	62.8	YES
2	40	35.4	NO
3	2	1.8	xMISSING

Table 60

62: Did anyone in you unit ever physically assault
a warrant officer? (ASWAR)

1. Yes   (YES)
2. No   (NO)
3. Not applicable (NA)

ASWAR = Assault a warrant officer

RANGE	FREQ	%	SG
1	41	36.3	YES
2	63	55.8	NO
3	9	8.0	xMISSING

105

Table 61

63: Have you heard stories about other units where officers have been assaulted? (ASTOR)

1. Yes   (YES)
2. No   (NO)
3. Not applicable (NA)

ASTOR = Stories about assaults

RANGE	FREQ	%	SG
1	65	57. 5	YES
2	45	39. 8	NO
3	3	2. 7	xMISSING

Table 62

64: In your opinion, how well do you think your unit would have fought in actual combat? (FIGHT)

1. Very well   (VWELL)
2. Fairly well   (FAIR)
3. Moderately well (MDTLY)
4. Poorly   (POOR)
5. Very poorly   (VPOOR)
6. Not applicable   (NA)

FIGHT = How good unit in combat

RANGE	FREQ	%	SG
1	10	8. 8	VWELL
2	41	36. 3	FAIR
3	38	33. 6	MDTLY
4	16	14. 2	POOR
5	2	1. 8	VPOOR
6	6	5. 3	xNA

Table 63

65: Did your officers seem to care very much about the
morale of your unit? (MORALE)

     1. Yes   (YES)
     2. No   (NO)
     3. Not applicable (NA)

MORALE = Officers care about morale

RANGE	FREQ	%	SG
1	66	58.4	YES
2	43	38.1	NO
3	4	3.5	xMISSING

Table 64

66: In your experience would you say that soldiers drink
more in the military than in civilian life? (DRINK)

     1. More in the military (MIL)
     2. More in civilian life (CIV)
     3. Not applicable   (NA)

DRINK = Drink more mil/civ

RANGE	FREQ	%	SG
1	31	27.4	MIL
2	78	69.0	CIV
3	4	3.5	xNA

<u>Table 65</u>

67: Do officers drink heavily? (OFDNK)

      1. Yes   (YES)
      2. No   (NO)
      3. Not applicable (NA)

OFDNK = Officer drinking habits

RANGE	FREQ	%	SG
1	95	84.1	YES
2	12	10.6	NO
3	6	5.3	xMISSING

<u>Table 66</u>

68: Did you ever hear of or see an officer drunk on
duty? (DRUNK)

      1. Yes   (YES)
      2. No   (NO)
      3. Not applicable (NA)

DRUNK = Officer drunk

RANGE	FREQ	%	SG
1	63	55.8	YES
2	46	40.7	NO
3	4	3.5	xMISSING

Table 67

69: Did you ever hear of or see an non-commissioned
officer drunk on duty? (NCODNK)

1. Yes   (YES)
2. No   (NO)
3. Not applicable (NA)

NCODNK = NCO drunk

RANGE	FREQ	%	SG
1	73	64.6	YES
2	34	30.1	NO
3	6	5.3	xMISSING

Table 68

70: How often are ordinary soldiers drinking or drunk
while on duty? (SOLDNK)

1. Very often   (VOFTEN)
2. Often   (OFTEN)
3. Seldom   (SELDOM)
4. Rarely   (RARELY)
5. Almost never (ALNEV)
6. Not applicable (NA)

SOLDNK = Often soldier drunk

RANGE	FREQ	%	SG
1	6	5.3	VOFTEN
2	12	10.6	OFTEN
3	29	25.7	SELDOM
4	30	26.5	RARELY
5	32	28.3	ALNEV
6	4	3.5	xNA

Table 69

71: Do superior officers regard excessive drinking as
      a major problem in the military? (EXDNK)

        1. Yes   (YES)
        2. No   (NO)
        3. Not applicable (NA)

EXDNK = Excess drinking prob

RANGE	FREQ	%	SG
1	75	66.4	YES
2	31	27.4	NO
3	7	6.2	xMISSING

Table 70

72: Did the amount of drinking in your unit affect the
      ability of your unit to perform its mission? (DNKPER)

        1. Yes   (YES)
        2. No   (NO)
        3. Not applicable (NA)

DNKPER = Drinking/unit perform

RANGE	FREQ	%	SG
1	34	30.1	YES
2	70	61.9	NO
3	9	8.0	xMISSING

Table 71

73: Are the punishments for drinking on duty severe or
generally lenient? (PUNDNK)

    1. Severe   (SEVERE)
    2. Lenient   (EASY)
    3. Not applicable (NA)

PUNDNK = Punishment for drink

RANGE	FREQ	%	SG
1	94	83. 2	SEVERE
2	10	8. 8	LENIENT
3	9	8. 0	xNA

Table 72

74: In your experience in the military were certain
national and religious groups singled out for
unfair treatment? (ETHNIC)

    1. Yes   (YES)
    2. No   (NO)
    3. Not applicable (NA)

ETHNIC = Unfair treatment

RANGE	FREQ	%	SG
1	78	69. 0	YES
2	32	28. 3	NO
3	3	2. 7	xMISSING

Table 73

75: Was this a common practice? (COMETH)

    1. Yes   (YES)
    2. No   (NO)
    3. Not applicable (NA)

COMETH = Unfair/ethnic/common

RANGE	FREQ	%	SG
1	64	56. 6	YES
2	36	31. 9	NO
3	13	11. 5	xMISSING

Table 74

76: How often do more experienced soldiers treat new
    recruits unfairly? (RECRU)

    1. Very often (VOFTEN)
    2. Often   (OFTEN)
    3. Seldom   (SELDOM)
    4. Rarely   (RARELY)
    5. Almost never (ALNEV)
    6. Not applicable (NA)

RECRU = Treat recruit unfair

RANGE	FREQ	%	SG
1	42	37. 2	VOFTEN
2	36	31. 9	OFTEN
3	23	20. 4	SELDOM
4	4	3. 5	RARELY
5	3	2. 7	ALNEV
6	5	4. 4	xNA

Table 75

77: Does this have a negative effect on the soldiers
morale? (NEGEF)

```
        1. Yes            (YES)
        2. No             (NO)
        3. Not applicable (NA)
```

NEGEF = Neg. effect on morale

RANGE	FREG	%	SG
1	86	76.1	YES
2	19	16.8	NO
3	8	7.1	xMISSING

Table 76

78: Are the officers aware of the unfair treatment that
soldiers receive from other older soldiers? (AWARE)

```
        1. Yes            (YES)
        2. No             (NO)
        3. Not applicable (NA)
```

AWARE = Officer aware/unfair

RANGE	FREG	%	SG
1	95	84.1	YES
2	10	8.8	NO
3	8	7.1	xMISSING

113

Table 77

79: How often do sargents treat the troops unfairly?
(SGTUN)

1. Very often   (VYOFT)
2. Often   (OFTEN)
3. Seldom   (SELDOM)
4. Rarely   (RARELY)
5. Almost never   (ALNEV)
6. Not applicable (NA)

SGTUN = Sgt. unfair treatment

RANGE	FREQ	%	SG
1	27	23.9	VOFTEN
2	37	32.7	OFTEN
3	33	29.2	SELDOM
4	8	7.1	RARELY
5	3	2.7	ALNEV
6	5	4.4	xNA

Table 78

80: In general do soldiers feel that they can go to
their officers or sargents with a complaint about
being treated unfairly? (SUPGO)

1. Yes   (YES)
2. No   (NO)
3. Not applicable (NA)

SUPGO = Go to superiors/unfair

RANGE	FREQ	%	SG
1	38	33.6	YES
2	72	63.7	NO
3	3	2.7	xMISSING

Table   79

81: Generally do most civilians treat soldiers well
    when the soldier is away from his base? (TREAT)

        1. Yes   (YES)
        2. No   (NO)
        3. Not applicable (NA)

TREAT = Civilian treat soldiers

RANGE	FREQ	%	SG
1	92	81.4	YES
2	16	14.2	NO
3	5	4.4	xMISSING

Table 80

82: In your opinion, how important do you think that
    belief in an ideology--Marxism-Leninism is in
    motivating a soldier to fight well? (IDEOL)

        1. The most important factor   (MOST)
        2. A very important factor   (VERY)
        3. Not very important at all   (NOTIMP)
        4. Almost totally unimportant (UNIMP)
        5. Not applicable

IDEOL = Ideology as motivator

RANGE	FREQ	%	SG
1	10	8.8	MOST
2	11	9.7	VERY
3	19	16.8	NOTIMP
4	71	62.8	UNIMP
5	2	1.8	xNA

Table 81

83: Which of the following things do you think is
most important to motivating a soldier to fight well?
(MOTIV)

1. Close ties to his comrades in the unit (TIES)
2. Support of the friends back home (HOME)
3. Feeling that one's officers/nco's care about you (CARE)
4. Belief in an ideology (IDEO)
5. Not wanting to appear a coward in front of your friends (NOCOW)
6. Not applicable (NA)

MOTIV = Factors motivating sold

RANGE	FREQ	%	SG
1	23	20.4	TIES
2	19	16.8	HOME
3	5	4.4	CARE
4	12	10.6	IDEO
5	50	44.2	NOCOW
6	4	3.5	xNA

Table 82

84: When you were in the military did anyone in your
unit ever commit suicide? (KILL)

1. Yes (YES)
2. No (NO)
3. Not applicable (NA)

KILL = Commit suicide

RANGE	FREQ	%	SG
1	55	48.7	YES
2	56	49.6	NO
3	2	1.8	xMISSING

Table 83

85: Did anyone in your unit ever attempt to commit
            suicide? (ATKIL)

    1. Yes   (YES)
    2. No   (NO)
    3. Not applicable (NA)

ATKILL = Attempted suicide

```
RANGE  FREQ    %    SG
==================================
  1     60   53. 1  YES
  2     47   41. 6  NO
  3      6    5. 3  xMISSING
```

Table 84

86: Did you ever hear stories about people committing
            suicide in other units? (STORSU)

    1. Yes   (YES)
    2. No   (NO)
    3. Not applicable (NA)

STORSU = Suicide stories/units

```
RANGE  FREQ    %    SG
==================================
  1     95   84. 1  YES
  2     16   14. 2  NO
  3      2    1. 8  xMISSING
```

Table 85

87: How common were the stories about suicide and
suicide attempts? (COMSTO)

1. Very common   (VCOMM)
2. Common   (COMM)
3. Generally uncommon (UNCOMM)
4. Fairly rare   (RARE)
5. Almost never   (ALNEV)
6. Not applicable   (NA)

COMSTO = Suicide stories/common

RANGE	FREQ	%	SG
1	7	6.2	VCOMM
2	17	15.0	COMM
3	20	17.7	UNCOMM
4	44	38.9	RARE
5	19	16.8	ALNEV
6	6	5.3	xNA

Table 86

88: In your experience whenever you heard about suicide
in the military did it happen most when: (WHENSU)

1. The soldier first came into the army (FIRST)
2. After he had been with his unit for awhile
(UNIT)
3. Not applicable (NA)

WHENSU = When suicide/attempts

RANGE	FREQ	%	SG
1	27	23.9	FIRST
2	67	59.3	UNIT
3	19	16.8	xNA

Table 87

89: Whenever you heard stories about suicide or suicide attempts, were there stories about officers as well? (OFFSU)

    1. Yes   (YES)
    2. No   (NO)
    3. Not applicable (NA)

OFFSU = Officers suicide

RANGE	FREQ	%	SG
1	32	28.3	YES
2	66	58.4	NO
3	15	13.3	xMISSING

Table 88

90: Non-commissioned officers? (NCOSU)

    1. Yes   (YES)
    2. No   (NO)
    3. Not applicable (NA)

NCOSU = NCO suicide

RANGE	FREQ	%	SG
1	63	55.8	YES
2	30	26.5	NO
3	20	17.7	xMISSING

Table 89

91: Warrant officers? (WARSU)

      1. Yes   (YES)
      2. No   (NO)
      3. Not applicable (NA)

WARSU = Warrant officer suicide

RANGE	FREQ	%	SG
1	18	15.9	YES
2	72	63.7	NO
3	23	20.4	xMISSING

Table 90

92: Is it true that many suicide attempts are actually attempts to get a release from military service? (SUREL)

      1. Yes   (YES)
      2. No   (NO)
      3. Not applicable (NA)

SUREL = Suicide for release

RANGE	FREQ	%	SG
1	55	48.7	YES
2	35	31.0	NO
3	23	20.4	xMISSING

Table 91

93: In your experience, were your superiors concerned
about the problem of suicide? (SUCARE)

        1. Yes   (YES)
        2. No   (NO)
        3. Not applicable (NA)

SUCARE = Superiors care/suicide

RANGE FREQ   %   SG
==================================
  1   54   47.8 YES
  2   40   35.4 NO
  3   19   16.8 xMISSING

Table 92

98: Given the general quality of officers that you
served within your military service, how would
you rate their quality as officers? (OFQUAL)

        1. Extremely good (EXGOOD)
        2. Good   (GOOD)
        3. Average   (AVG)
        4. Fair   (FAIR)
        5. Poor   (POOR)
        6. Very poor   (VYPOOR)
        7. Not applicable (NA)

OFQUAL = Officer quality

RANGE FREQ   %   SG
==================================
  1   1   0.9 EXGOOD
  2   11   9.7 GOOD
  3   64   56.6 AVG
  4   16   14.2 FAIR
  5   17   15.0 POOR
  6   2   1.8 VPOOR
  7   2   1.8 xNA

121

Table 93

99: How would you rate the quality of the non-commissioned officers you came into contact with? (NCOQUAL)

        1. Extremely good (EXGOOD)
        2. Good   (GOOD)
        3. Average   (AVER)
        4. Fair   (FAIR)
        5. Poor   (POOR)
        6. Very poor   (VYPOR)
        7. Not applicable (NA)

NCOQUAL = NCO quality

RANGE	FREQ	%	SG
1	2	1.8	EXGOOD
2	21	18.6	GOOD
3	50	44.2	AVG
4	23	20.4	FAIR
5	10	8.8	POOR
6	5	4.4	VPOOR
7	2	1.8	xNA

Table 94

100: How close to your fellow soldiers did you feel when you were in the military? (CLOFEL)

        1. Very close   (VCLOSE)
        2. Close   (CLOSE)
        3. Moderately close   (MCLOSE)
        4. Not close at all   (NCLOSE)
        5. I felt few bonds with them (FEW)
        6. Not applicable   (NA)

CLOFEL = Close with comrades

RANGE	FREQ	%	SG
1	6	5.3	VCLOSE
2	16	14.2	CLOSE
3	33	29.2	MCLOSE
4	21	18.6	NCLOSE
5	35	31.0	FEW
6	2	1.8	xNA

Table 95

101: How strongly did you develop feelings of pride and
affection for your military unit? (PRIDE)

        1. Very strongly   (VYSTR)
        2. Strongly   (STRNG)
        3. Moderately   (MDTY)
        4. Not very strong   (NOSTG)
        5. Unit pride did not concern me much   (NOCON)
        6. No feelings of pride at all   (NOPRD)
        7. Not applicable   (NA)

PRIDE = Pride in military unit

RANGE	FREQ	%	SG
1	2	1.8	VSTR
2	5	4.4	STRONG
3	9	8.0	MDTY
4	28	24.8	NVSTR
5	25	22.1	NCON
6	42	37.2	NPRIDE
7	2	1.8	xNA

Table 96

102: When you were in the military did anyone in your
unit ever desert? (DSRT)

        1. Yes   (YES)
        2. No   (NO)
        3. Not applicable (NA)

DSRT = Desertion

RANGE	FREQ	%	SG
1	56	49.6	YES
2	53	46.9	NO
3	4	3.5	xMISSING

Table 97

103: Did you ever hear of an officer deserting? (OFFDRT)

1. Yes   (YES)
2. No   (NO)
3. Not applicable (NA)

OFFDRT = Officer desertion

RANGE	FREQ	%	SG
1	17	15. 0	YES
2	92	81. 4	NO
3	4	3. 5	xMISSING

Table 98

104: Did you ever hear of a warrant officer deserting?
(WARDRT)

1. Yes   (YES)
2. No   (NO)
3. Not applicable (NA)

WARDRT = Warrant officer desertion

RANGE	FREQ	%	SG
1	11	9. 7	YES
2	91	80. 5	NO
3	11	9. 7	xMISSING

Table 99

105: Did you ever hear of a non-commissioned officer
          deserting? (NCODRT)

          1. Yes   (YES)
          2. No   (NO)
          3. Not applicable (NA)

NCODRT = NCO desertion

RANGE	FREQ	%	SG
1	72	63.7	YES
2	38	33.6	NO
3	3	2.7	xMISSING

Table 100

106: In general, were the stories that you heard about
          soldiers deserting, (DRTCOM)

          1. Very common   (VCOMM)
          2. Common   (COMM)
          3. Generally uncommon   (GUNCOM)
          4. Rare   (RARE)
          5. Almost never heard such stories (ALNEV)
          6. Not applicable   (NA)

DRTCOM = Commoness of desertion

RANGE	FREQ	%	SG
1	8	7.1	VCOMM
2	19	16.8	COMM
3	5	4.4	GUNCOMM
4	53	46.9	RARE
5	25	22.1	ALNEV
6	3	2.7	xNA

Table 101

107: How often did soldiers in your unit go absent
without leave? (AWOL)

1. Quite often   (QOFT)
2. Often   (OFTEN)
3. Fairly often   (FAOFT)
4. Not very much (NOMCH)
5. Rarely   (RARE)
6. Almost never   (ALNEV)
7. Not applicable (NA)

AWOL = AWOL rate

RANGE	FREQ	%	SG
1	32	28.3	QOFTEN
2	24	21.2	OFTEN
3	24	21.2	FOFTEN
4	15	13.3	NVMUCH
5	12	10.6	RARE
6	5	4.4	ALNEV
7	1	0.9	xNA

Table 102

108: What are some of the reasons that soldiers tried
to go absent without leave? (WOLREA)

1. To get vodka   (VODKA)
2. To meet women   (WOMEN)
3. To escape military life for a short time (ESCL
4. To try to get away from the military for good
   (ESCGD)
5. Family problems   (FAMILY)
6. Unfair treatment by superiors   (TREAT)
7. To buy some extra food   (FOOD)
8. To get some drugs   (DRUGS)
9. Not applicable   (NA)

WOLREA = Reasons for AWOL

RANGE	FREQ	%	SG
1	94	83.2	VODKA
2	7	6.2	WOMEN
3	6	5.3	ESCLIF
4	0	0.0	ESCGD
5	0	0.0	FAMILY
6	0	0.0	TREAT
7	0	0.0	FOOD
8	1	0.9	DRUGS
9	5	4.4	xNA

WOLREB = REasons for AWOL (2)

RANGE	FREQ	%	SG
1	1	0.9	VODKA
2	87	77.0	WOMEN
3	10	8.8	ESCLIF
4	0	0.0	ESCGD
5	1	0.9	FAMILY
6	2	1.8	TREAT
7	0	0.0	FOOD
8	0	0.0	DRUGS
9	12	10.6	xNA

WOLREC = Reasons for AWOL (3)

RANGE	FREQ	%	SG
1	1	0.9	VODKA
2	0	0.0	WOMEN
3	47	41.6	ESCLIF
4	0	0.0	ESCGD
5	14	12.4	FAMILY
6	2	1.8	TREAT
7	30	26.5	FOOD
8	2	1.8	DRUGS
9	17	15.0	xNA

Table 103

109: Were your superiors concerned with the problem
of soldiers going absent without leave? (WOLCO)

```
1. Yes          (YES)
2. No           (NO)
3. Not applicable (NA)
```

WOLCO = Superiors concern/AWOL

RANGE	FREQ	%	SG
1	79	69.9	YES
2	27	23.9	NO
3	7	6.2	xMISSING

Table 104

110: Were they concerned with the problem of desertion?
(SUPDRT)

1. Yes
2. No
3. Not applicable (NA)

SUPDRT = Superiors concern/Desertion

RANGE	FREQ	%	SG
1	73	64.6	YES
2	30	26.5	NO
3	10	8.8	xMISSING

Table 105

111: In general, is going absent without leave a big
problem in the military? (PROBA)

1. Yes	(YES)
2. No	(NO)
3. Not applicable	(NA)

PROBA = AWOL a big problem

RANGE	FREQ	%	SG
1	87	77.0	YES
2	20	17.7	NO
3	6	5.3	xMISSING

Table 106

112: Is desertion a big problem in the military? (PROBD)

```
         1. Yes            (YES)
         2. No             (NO)
         3. Not applicable (NA)
```

PROBD = Desertion a big problem

RANGE	FREQ	%	SG
1	54	47.8	YES
2	51	45.1	NO
3	8	7.1	xMISSING

Table 107

113: Is the punishment for going absent without leave
       harsh or lenient? (AWOLP)

```
         1. Harsh          (HARSH)
         2. Lenient        (EASY)
         3. Not applicable (NA)
```

AWOLP = Punishment for AWOL

RANGE	FREQ	%	SG
1	93	82.3	HARSH
2	17	15.0	EASY
3	3	2.7	xNA

Table 108

114: Was genuinely interested in his men's personal
problems. (INPER)

1. Officer   (OFF)
2. Non-commissioned officer   (NCO)
3. Warrant officer   (WAR)
4. All three   (ALL)
5. Not applicable   (NA)

INPER = Interested/personal problem

RANGE	FREQ	%	SG
1	31	27.4	OFF
2	12	10.6	NCO
3	1	0.9	WAR
4	5	4.4	ALL
5	64	56.6	xNA

Table 109

115: Went out of his way to show an interest in his
men. (SHOINT)

1. Officer   (OFF)
2. Non-commissioned officer   (NCO)
3. Warrant officer   (WAR)
4. All three   (ALL)
5. Not applicable   (NA)

SHOINT = Shows interest in men

RANGE	FREQ	%	SG
1	22	19.5	OFF
2	8	7.1	NCO
3	4	3.5	WAR
4	10	8.8	ALL
5	69	61.1	xNA

Table 110

116: Seemed more concerned with his own career advance-
        ment than with his men. (CARADV)

        1. Officer   (OFF)
        2. Non-commissioned officer   (NCO)
        3. Warrant officer   (WAR)
        4. All three   (ALL)
        5. Not applicable   (NA)

CARADV = Career advancement

RANGE	FREQ	%	SG
1	37	32.7	OFF
2	11	9.7	NCO
3	6	5.3	WAR
4	45	39.8	ALL
5	14	12.4	xNA

Table 111

117: He treated people in an impersonal manner--
        like cogs in a machine. (COGS)

        1. Officer   (OFF)
        2. Non-commissioned officer   (NCO)
        3. Warrant officer   (WAR)
        4. All three   (ALL)
        5. Not applicable   (NA)

COGS = Treated men impersonaly

RANGE	FREQ	%	SG
1	30	26.5	OFF
2	8	7.1	NCO
3	7	6.2	WAR
4	42	37.2	ALL
5	26	23.0	xNA

Table 112

118: Stood up for his men when dealing with his
superiors. (STODUP)

1. Officer   (OFF)
2. Non-commissioned officer   (NCO)
3. Warrant officer   (WAR)
4. All three   (ALL)
5. Not applicable   (NA)

STODUP = Stood up for his men

RANGE	FREQ	%	SG
1	20	17.7	OFF
2	11	9.7	NCO
3	7	6.2	WAR
4	10	8.8	ALL
5	65	57.5	xNA

Table 113

120: Shared hardships with his troops. (HARSHP)

1. Officer   (OFF)
2. Non-commissioned officer   (NCO)
3. Warrant officer   (WAR)
4. All three   (ALL)
5. Not applicable   (NA)

HARSHP = Shared hardship with men

RANGE	FREQ	%	SG
1	7	6.2	OFF
2	26	23.0	NCO
3	5	4.4	WAR
4	18	15.9	ALL
5	57	50.4	xNA

132

Table 114

121: Saw to it that his men had the things they needed
in military life. (HADTHI)

```
            1. Officer                  (OFF)
            2. Non-commissioned officer (NCO)
            3. Warrant officer          (WAR)
            4. All three                (ALL)
            5. Not applicable           (NA)
```

HADTHI = Men got what needed

RANGE	FREQ	%	SG
1	22	19.5	OFF
2	10	8.8	NCO
3	12	10.6	WAR
4	20	17.7	ALL
5	49	43.4	xNA

Table 115

122: Always set the example for his men. (EXAMP)

```
            1. Officer                  (OFF)
            2. Non-commissioned officer (NCO)
            3. Warrant officer          (WAR)
            4. All three                (ALL)
            5. Not applicable           (NA)
```

EXAMP = Set example for men

RANGE	FREQ	%	SG
1	18	15.9	OFF
2	9	8.0	NCO
3	3	2.7	WAR
4	9	8.0	ALL
5	74	65.5	xNA

Table 116

123: Drew too strong a line between himself and his men;
he was too distant. (DIST)

        1. Officer   (OFF)
        2. Non-commissioned officer   (NCO)
        3. Warrant officer   (WAR)
        4. All three   (ALL)
        5. Not applicable   (NA)

DIST = Was too distant

RANGE	FREG	%	SG
1	41	36.3	OFF
2	8	7.1	NCO
3	7	6.2	WAR
4	31	27.4	ALL
5	26	23.0	xNA

Table 117

124: Had the kind of judgement I would trust in
combat. (JUDGE)

        1. Officer   (OFF)
        2. Non-commissioned officer   (NCO)
        3. Warrant officer   (WAR)
        4. All three   (ALL)
        5. Not applicable   (NA)

JUDGE = Had judgement/combat

RANGE	FREG	%	SG
1	21	18.6	OFF
2	9	8.0	NCO
3	1	0.9	WAR
4	7	6.2	ALL
5	75	66.4	xNA

Table 118

125: Truly knew his men and respected their capabilities.
(KNEWRE)

        1. Officer   (OFF)
        2. Non-commissioned officer (NCO)
        3. Warrant officer   (WAR)
        4. All three   (ALL)
        5. Not applicable   (NA)

KNEWRE = Knew men/respect cap

RANGE	FREQ	%	SG
1	21	18. 6	OFF
2	8	7. 1	NCO
3	7	6. 2	WAR
4	12	10. 6	ALL
5	65	57. 5	xNA

Table 119

126: Never developed personal ties with his men. (NOPETI)

        1. Officer   (OFF)
        2. Non-commissioned officer (NCO)
        3. Warrant officer   (WAR)
        4. All three   (ALL)
        5. Not applicable   (NA)

NOPETI = No personal ties

RANGE	FREQ	%	SG
1	26	23. 0	OFF
2	6	5. 3	NCO
3	4	3. 5	WAR
4	30	26. 5	ALL
5	47	41. 6	xNA

Table 120

127: He was concerned about the unit's morale and did
everything he could to make it high. (MORHI)

      1. Officer   (OFF)
      2. Non-commissioned officer (NCO)
      3. Warrant officer   (WAR)
      4. All three   (ALL)
      5. Not applicable   (NA)

MORHI = Made morale high

RANGE	FREQ	%	SG
1	31	27.4	OFF
2	3	2.7	NCO
3	3	2.7	WAR
4	20	17.7	ALL
5	56	49.6	xNA

Table 121

128: Often tried to avoid taking responsibility when
things went wrong. (WRONG)

      1. Officer   (OFF)
      2. Non-commissioned officer (NCO)
      3. Warrant officer   (WAR)
      4. All three   (ALL)
      5. Not applicable   (NA)

WRONG = Avoided responsibility

RANGE	FREQ	%	SG
1	18	15.9	OFF
2	14	12.4	NCO
3	5	4.4	WAR
4	49	43.4	ALL
5	27	23.9	xNA

Table 122

129: Listened with genuine sympathy to the problems
of the troops. (SYMLIS)

1. Officer   (OFF)
2. Non-commissioned officer   (NCO)
3. Warrant officer   (WAR)
4. All three   (ALL)
5. Not applicable   (NA)

SYMLIS = Listened to problems

RANGE	FREQ	%	SG
1	16	14.2	OFF
2	7	6.2	NCO
3	4	3.5	WAR
4	8	7.1	ALL
5	78	69.0	xNA

Table 123

130: Often praised his troops for doing a good job
and meant it. (PRAISE)

1. Officer   (OFF)
2. Non-commissioned officer   (NCO)
3. Warrant officer   (WAR)
4. All three   (ALL)
5. Not applicable   (NA)

PRAISE = Praised troops/good job

RANGE	FREQ	%	SG
1	28	24.8	OFF
2	6	5.3	NCO
3	3	2.7	WAR
4	14	12.4	ALL
5	62	54.9	xNA

137

Table 124

131: Would make a good man to go into combat with.
(COMGUD)

        1. Officer   (OFF)
        2. Non-commissioned officer (NCO)
        3. Warrant officer   (WAR)
        4. All three   (ALL)
        5. Not applicable   (NA)

COMGUD = Good man in combat

RANGE	FREQ	%	SG
1	19	16.8	OFF
2	14	12.4	NCO
3	2	1.8	WAR
4	3	2.7	ALL
5	75	66.4	xNA

Table 125

132: He would probably distort reports to make himself
look better. (DISTO)

        1. Officer   (OFF)
        2. Non-commissioned officer (NCO)
        3. Warrant officer   (WAR)
        4. All three   (ALL)
        5. Not applicable   (NA)

DISTO = Distort reports/career

RANGE	FREQ	%	SG
1	11	9.7	OFF
2	13	11.5	NCO
3	9	8.0	WAR
4	42	37.2	ALL
5	38	33.6	xNA

138

Table 126

133: He was overly ambitious at the expense of his
        subordinates and his unit. (OVAMB)

1. Officer	(OFF)
2. Non-commissioned officer	(NCO)
3. Warrant officer	(WAR)
4. All three	(ALL)
5. Not applicable	(NA)

OVAMB = Overly ambitious

RANGE	FREQ	%	SG
1	20	17.7	OFF
2	10	8.8	NCO
3	10	8.8	WAR
4	38	33.6	ALL
5	35	31.0	xNA

Table 127

134: Tended to concentrate on the small unimportant
        things. (UNIMP)

1. Officer	(OFF)
2. Non-commissioned officer	(NCO)
3. Warrant officer	(WAR)
4. All three	(ALL)
5. Not applicable	(NA)

UNIMP = Looks at small things

RANGE	FREQ	%	SG
1	11	9.7	OFF
2	17	15.0	NCO
3	12	10.6	WAR
4	33	29.2	ALL
5	40	35.4	xNA

Table 128

135: Encouraged strong ties with the military unit. (UTIE

```
        1. Officer                     (OFF)
        2. Non-commissioned officer    (NCO)
        3. Warrant officer             (WAR)
        4. All three                   (ALL)
        5. Not applicable              (NA)
```

UTIES = Made strong unit ties

RANGE	FREQ	%	SG
1	32	28.3	OFF
2	3	2.7	NCO
3	6	5.3	WAR
4	18	15.9	ALL
5	54	47.8	xNA

Table 129

136: Used his position to take advantage of other
soldiers. (USEPO)

```
        1. Officer                     (OFF)
        2. Non-commissioned officer    (NCO)
        3. Warrant officer             (WAR)
        4. All three                   (ALL)
        5. Not applicable              (NA)
```

USEPO = Used position/take advantage

RANGE	FREQ	%	SG
1	15	13.3	OFF
2	10	8.8	NCO
3	12	10.6	WAR
4	46	40.7	ALL
5	30	26.5	xNA

Table 130

137: Stifled the initiative of others. (STIFLE)

```
        1. Officer                     (OFF)
        2. Non-commissioned officer    (NCO)
        3. Warrant officer             (WAR)
        4. All three                   (ALL)
        5. Not applicable              (NA)
```

STIFLE = Stifled initiative

RANGE	FREQ	%	SG
1	13	11.5	OFF
2	10	8.8	NCO
3	8	7.1	WAR
4	30	26.5	ALL
5	52	46.0	xNA

Table 131

138: He was willing to support his subordinates when
        they made mistakes. (MISTKE)

```
        1. Officer                     (OFF)
        2. Non-commissioned officer    (NCO)
        3. Warrant officer             (WAR)
        4. All three                   (ALL)
        5. Not applicable              (NA)
```

MISTKE = Support men when mistakes

RANGE	FREQ	%	SG
1	10	8.8	OFF
2	5	4.4	NCO
3	0	0.0	WAR
4	9	8.0	ALL
5	89	78.8	xNA

Table 132

139: Seemed more concerned about the troops than his
own advancement. (TRPCON)

        1. Officer   (OFF)
        2. Non-commissioned officer   (NCO)
        3. Warrant officer   (WAR)
        4. All three   (ALL)
        5. Not applicable   (NA)

TRPCON = Concerned about troops more

RANGE	FREQ	%	SG
1	6	5.3	OFF
2	3	2.7	NCO
3	0	0.0	WAR
4	7	6.2	ALL
5	97	85.8	xNA

Table 133

140: He would hesitate to take actions in the absence
of instructions from his superiors. (HESIT)

        1. Officer   (OFF)
        2. Non-commissioned officer   (NCO)
        5. Warrant officer   (WAR)
        4. All three   (ALL)
        5. Not applicable   (NA)

HESIT = Hesitate to act

RANGE	FREQ	%	SG
1	12	10.6	OFF
2	11	9.7	NCO
3	7	6.2	WAR
4	46	40.7	ALL
5	37	32.7	xNA

Table 134

141: Tended to limit his contact with his men. (LIMCON)

     1. Officer   (OFF)
     2. Non-commissioned officer (NCO)
     3. Warrant officer   (WAR)
     4. All three   (ALL)
     5. Not applicable   (NA)

LIMCON = Limit contact with men

RANGE	FREQ	%	SG
1	35	31.0	OFF
2	6	5.3	NCO
3	3	2.7	WAR
4	26	23.0	ALL
5	43	38.1	xNA

Table 135

142: He was generally available to his men to deal
with their personal problems. (PERPRO)

     1. Officer   (OFF)
     2. Non-commissioned officer (NCO)
     3. Warrant officer   (WAR)
     4. All three   (ALL)
     5. Not applicable   (NA)

PPROB = Available/personal prob

RANGE	FREQ	%	SG
1	12	10.6	OFF
2	9	8.0	NCO
3	6	5.3	WAR
4	21	18.6	ALL
5	65	57.5	xNA

Table 136

143: He was a good example to young soldiers. (GOODEX)

1. Officer   (OFF)
2. Non-commissioned officer (NCO)
3. Warrant officer   (WAR)
4. All three   (ALL)
5. Not applicable   (NA)

GOODEX = Good example for men

RANGE	FREQ	%	SG
1	14	12.4	OFF
2	17	15.0	NCO
3	4	3.5	WAR
4	9	8.0	ALL
5	69	61.1	xNA

Table 137

144: Helped men overcome their lack of confidence.
(LACKCO)

1. Officer   (OFF)
2. Non-commissioned officer (NCO)
3. Warrant officer   (WAR)
4. All three   (ALL)
5. Not applicable   (NA)

LACKCO = Overcome lack of confidence

RANGE	FREQ	%	SG
1	12	10.6	OFF
2	17	15.0	NCO
3	9	8.0	WAR
4	13	11.5	ALL
5	62	54.9	xNA

Table 138

145: He was selfish. (SELF)

    1. Officer   (OFF)
    2. Non-commissioned officer   (NCO)
    3. Warrant officer   (WAR)
    4. All three   (ALL)
    5. Not applicable   (NA)

SELF = Selfish person

RANGE	FREQ	%	SG
1	12	10.6	OFF
2	7	6.2	NCO
3	6	5.3	WAR
4	50	44.2	ALL
5	38	33.6	xNA

Table 139

146: Tended to blame others for things he was supposed to do when they went wrong. (BLAME)

    1. Officer   (OFF)
    2. Non-commissioned officer   (NCO)
    3. Warrant officer   (WAR)
    4. All three   (ALL)
    5. Not applicable   (NA)

BLAME = Blame others for errors

RANGE	FREQ	%	SG
1	11	9.7	OFF
2	11	9.7	NCO
3	9	8.0	WAR
4	44	38.9	ALL
5	38	33.6	xNA

<u>Table 140</u>

147: Stuck to the letter of his superiors orders.
(STUCK)

     1. Officer   (OFF)
     2. Non-commissioned officer (NCO)
     3. Warrant officer   (WAR)
     4. All three   (ALL)
     5. Not applicable   (NA)

STUCK = Stuck to letter orders

RANGE	FREQ	%	SG
1	16	14.2	OFF
2	6	5.3	NCO
3	6	5.3	WAR
4	51	45.1	ALL
5	34	30.1	xNA

<u>Table 141</u>

150: In general, were conscript non-commissioned officers better than professional non-commissioned officers. (WHOBET)

     1. Yes
     2. No
     3. Not applicable (NA)

WHOBET = Who was better

RANGE	FREQ	%	SG
1	54	47.8	YES
2	7	6.2	NO
3 - 5	52	46.0	xNA

Table 142

151: On a scale from 1 to 10 in which 1 is the worst and 10 is the best, how well do you think your unit would do in actual combat? (SCALCO)

1	2	3	4	5	6	7	8	9	10
Worst									Best

SCALCO = Scale of combat ability

RANGE	FREQ	%	SG
0	6	5.3	xNA
1	3	2.7	1
2	2	1.8	2
3	18	15.9	3
4	17	15.0	4
5	17	15.0	5
6	13	11.5	6
7	16	14.2	7
8	13	11.5	8
9	2	1.8	9
10	6	5.3	10

```
MEDIAN                           5
QUARTILES                 3           7
EXTREMES           0                      10

MEAN =  5.18584     STANDARD DEVIATION =  2.45876

NUMBER OF MISSING DATA VALUES:   0
MISSING DATA CODE(S): NONE
```

Table 143

152: About how many hours a week are spent in political subjects and ideological indoctrination? (INDOC)

INDOC = Hours a week/indoctrin

No mappings are saved for this variable

```
MEDIAN                           8
QUARTILES                 4          12
EXTREMES           0                      25

MEAN =  8.68142     STANDARD DEVIATION =  6.35451

NUMBER OF MISSING DATA VALUES:   0
MISSING DATA CODE(S): NONE
```

147

Table 144

153: Among the soldiers that you knew, do you think
that these kinds of classes are important in
making a soldier want to be a good soldier?
(CLASS)

           1. Yes   (YES)
           2. No   (NO)
           3. Not applicable (NA)

CLASS = Are indoc classes good

RANGE   FREQ   %   SG
=====================================
  1   23   20.4 YES
  2   85   75.2 NO
  3   5   4.4 xMISSING

Table 145

154: On a scale from 1 to 10 in which 1 is least impor-
tant and 10 is the most important, how important
is a soldier's belief in Marxism-Leninism in
motivating him to fight well? (MARX)

  1   2   3   4   5   6   7   8   9   10
Least important   Most important

MARX = Marxism as motivator

RANGE   FREQ   %   SG
=====================================
  0   4   3.5 xNA
  1   50   44.2 1
  2   18   15.9 2
  3   17   15.0 3
  4   4   3.5 4
  5   5   4.4 5
  6   2   1.8 6
  7   4   3.5 7
  8   3   2.7 8
  9   1   0.9 9
 10   5   4.4 10

MEDIAN   2
QUARTILES   1   3
EXTREMES   0   10

MEAN = 2.66372   STANDARD DEVIATION = 2.50575

NUMBER OF MISSING DATA VALUES: 0
MISSING DATA CODE(S): NONE

Table 146

155: Did Soviet officers make any effort to break up
strong personal ties between soldiers. (BRKFRI)

     1. Yes   (YES)
     2. No   (NO)
     3. Not applicable (NA)

BRKFRI = Break up friendships

    RANGE FREQ   %   SG
    ================================
      1   29   25. 7 YES
      2   69   61. 1 NO
      3   15   13. 3 xMISSING

Table 147

156: On a scale from 1 to 10 in which 1 is the worst
and 10 the best, how would you rate the military
training your unit received? (TRAIN)

    1   2   3   4   5   6   7   8   9   10
    Worst   Best

TRAIN = Quality of training

    RANGE   FREQ   %   SG
    ===================================
       0   5   4. 4 xNA
       1   6   5. 3 1
       2   8   7. 1 2
       3   14   12. 4 3
       4   9   8. 0 4
       5   20   17. 7 5
       6   7   6. 2 6
       7   18   15. 9 7
       8   16   14. 2 8
       9   3   2. 7 9
      10   7   6. 2 10

Table 148

Perceptions of the Combat Ability of Soviet
Units Over Time By Mean Scores Of A
Maximum Scale Score of 10

Time Period	N	Mean Score
Prewar	5	3.0
1940-1952	21	5.6
1953-1957	21	5.8
1958-1963	11	5.5
1964-1978	49	5.2

Table 149

Quality of Soviet Military Training
Over Time By Mean Score Of A
Maximum Scale Score of 10

Time Period	N	Mean Score
Prewar	6	5.1
1940-1952	24	5.5
1953-1957	31	5.9
1958-1963	11	6.2
1964-1978	50	4.8

Table 150

Periods of Service: pre-WW II (PREWAR), 1940-1952 (WAR), 1953-1957 (POSTA), 1958-1963 (CUBA), 1964-1978 (MOD) as a Background Variable for Question # 98

"Given the general quality of officers that you served with in your military service, how would you rate their quality as officers"

CATDAT BY OFQUAL

DOWN: Serv periods
ACROSS: Officer quality

PERCENTAGES ACROSS
========== ======

	EXGOOD	GOOD	AVG	FAIR	POOR	VPOOR	TOTAL
PREWAR	*	*	*	*	*	*	5
	0	0	5	0	0	0	
WAR	4. 3%	4. 3%	52. 2%	4. 3%	30. 4%	4. 3%	23
	1	1	12	1	7	1	
POSTA	0. 0%	14. 3%	57. 1%	19. 0%	9. 5%	0. 0%	21
	0	3	12	4	2	0	
CUBA	0. 0%	0. 0%	76. 9%	23. 1%	0. 0%	0. 0%	13
	0	0	10	3	0	0	
MOD	0. 0%	14. 3%	51. 0%	16. 3%	16. 3%	2. 0%	49
	0	7	25	8	8	1	
TOTAL	0. 9%	9. 9%	57. 7%	14. 4%	15. 3%	1. 8%	111
	1	11	64	16	17	2	

Exclusion analysis:
Table total: 111
Excluded: 2
Sample size: 113

Table 151

Periods of Service: pre-WW II (PREWAR), 1940-1952 (WAR),
1953-1957 (POSTA), 1958-1963 (CUBA), 1964-1978 (MOD) as
a Background Variable for Question # 99

"How would you rate the quality of non-commissioned
officers you came into contact with"

CATDAT BY NCOQUAL

DOWN: Serv periods
ACROSS: NCO quality

PERCENTAGES ACROSS
============ ======

	EXGOOD	GOOD	AVG	FAIR	POOR	VPOOR	TO
PREWAR	*	*	*	*	*	*	
	1	0	3	1	0	0	
WAR	4. 3%	21. 7%	47. 8%	13. 0%	4. 3%	8. 7%	
	1	5	11	3	1	2	
POSTA	0. 0%	19. 0%	33. 3%	33. 3%	14. 3%	0. 0%	
	0	4	7	7	3	0	
CUBA	0. 0%	15. 4%	76. 9%	0. 0%	7. 7%	0. 0%	
	0	2	10	0	1	0	
MOD	0. 0%	20. 4%	38. 8%	24. 5%	10. 2%	6. 1%	
	0	10	19	12	5	3	
TOTAL	1. 8%	18. 9%	45. 0%	20. 7%	9. 0%	4. 5%	
	2	21	50	23	10	5	

Exclusion analysis:
Table total: 111
Excluded: 2
Sample size: 113

Table 152

Periods of Service: pre-WW II (PREWAR), 1940-1952 (WAR), 1953-1957 (POSTA), 1958-1963 (CUBA), 1964-1978 (MOD), a Background Variable for Question # 151

"On a scale of from 1 to 10 in which 1 is the worst and 10 is the best, how well do you think your unit would do in actual combat"

CATDAT BY SCALCO

DOWN: Serv periods
ACROSS: Scale of combat ability

PERCENTAGES ACROSS

PREWAR	1	2	3	4	5	6	7	8	9	10	TOTAL
WAR	0.0% 0	0.0% 0	23.8% 5	19.0% 4	14.3% 3	9.5% 2	9.5% 2	4.8% 1	4.8% 1	14.3% 3	21
POSTA	4.8% 1	0.0% 0	9.5% 2	9.5% 2	14.3% 3	9.5% 2	33.3% 7	14.3% 3	4.8% 1	0.0% 0	21
CUBA	9.1% 1	0.0% 0	9.1% 1	0.0% 0	36.4% 4	9.1% 1	9.1% 1	27.3% 3	0.0% 0	0.0% 0	11
MOD	2.0% 1	4.1% 2	20.4% 10	20.4% 10	10.2% 5	12.2% 6	12.2% 6	12.2% 6	0.0% 0	6.1% 3	49
TOTAL	2.8% 3	1.9% 2	16.8% 18	15.9% 17	15.9% 17	12.1% 13	15.0% 16	12.1% 13	1.9% 2	5.6% 6	107

Exclusion analysis:
Table total: 107
Excluded: 6
Sample size: 113

153

Table 153

Periods of Service: pre-WW II (PREWAR), 1940-1952 (WAR),
1953-1957 (POSTA), 1958-1963 (CUBA), 1964-1978)MOD) as
a Background Variable for Question # 64

"In your opinion, how well do you think your unit would
have fought in actaul combat"

FIGHT BY CATDAT

DOWN: How good unit in combat
ACROSS: Serv periods

PERCENTAGES ACROSS

	PREWAR	WAR	POSTA	CUBA	MOD	TOTAL
VWELL	0. 0%	40. 0%	10. 0%	0. 0%	50. 0%	10
	0	4	1	0	5	
FAIR	7. 3%	22. 0%	24. 4%	17. 1%	29. 3%	41
	3	9	10	7	12	
MDTLY	5. 3%	15. 8%	23. 7%	7. 9%	47. 4%	38
	2	6	9	3	18	
POOR	0. 0%	18. 7%	0. 0%	12. 5%	68. 7%	16
	0	3	0	2	11	
VPOOR	*	*	*	*	*	2
	0	0	0	0	2	
TOTAL	4. 7%	20. 6%	18. 7%	11. 2%	44. 9%	107
	5	22	20	12	48	

Exclusion analysis:
Table total: 107
Excluded: 6
Sample size: 113

Table 154

Periods of Service: pre-WW II (PREWAR), 1940-1952 (WAR),
1953-1957 (POSTA), 1958-1963 (CUBA), 1964-1978 (MOD) as
a Background Variable for Question # 156

"On a scale of from 1 to 10 in which 1 is the worst and
10 is the best, how would you rate the miltary training
your unit received"

PREWAR	5.0	N-6
WAR	6.6	N-21
POSTA	5.8	N-30
CUBA	6.1	N-11
MOD	5.4	N-49

Table 155

Periods of Service: pre-WW II (PREWAR), 1940-1952 (WAR),
1953-1957 (POSTA), 1958-1963 (CUBA), 1964-1978 (MOD) as
a Background Variable for Question # 112

"Is desertion a big problem in the military"

CATDAT BY PROBD

DOWN: Serv periods
ACROSS: Desertion a big problem

PERCENTAGES ACROSS

	YES	NO	TOTAL
PREWAR	*	*	5
	5	0	
WAR	71.4%	28.6%	21
	15	6	
POSTA	45.0%	55.0%	20
	9	11	
CUBA	72.7%	27.3%	11
	8	3	
MOD	35.4%	64.6%	48
	17	31	
TOTAL	51.4%	48.6%	105
	54	51	

Exclusion analysis:
Table total: 105
Excluded: 8
Sample size: 113

Table 156

Periods of Service: pre-WW II (PREWAR), 1940-1952 (WAR), 1953-1957 (POSTA), 1958-1963 (CUBA), 1964-1978 (MOD) as a Background Variable for Question # 111

"In general, is going absent without leave a big problem in the military"

CATDAT BY PROBA

DOWN: Serv periods
ACROSS: AWOL a big problem

PERCENTAGES ACROSS

	YES	NO	TOTAL
PREWAR	*	*	5
	4	1	
WAR	81. 0%	19. 0%	21
	17	4	
POSTA	75. 0%	25. 0%	20
	15	5	
CUBA	91. 7%	8. 3%	12
	11	1	
MOD	81. 6%	18. 4%	49
	40	9	
TOTAL	81. 3%	18. 7%	107
	87	20	

Exclusion analysis:
Table total: 107
Excluded: 6
Sample size: 113

Table 157

Perceptions of the Combat Ability of Soviet
Units By Rank By Mean Scores Of A
Maximum Scale Score of 10

Rank	N	Mean Score
Private	55	4.6
Non-Commissioned officer	29	6.3
Officer	19	6.2

Table 158

Perceptions Of Quality Of Soviet Military
Training By Rank By Mean Score Of A
Maximum Scale Score Of 10

Rank	N	Mean Score
Private	56	4.8
Non-Commissioned Officer	29	6.7
Officer	19	5.8

Table 159

Perceptions Of Soviet Military Living Quarters By Rank

30: "In general, how would you describe the living
quarters you lived in while in the military?

RANK BY QTRS

DOWN: Highest rank
ACROSS: Living quarters

	PERCENTAGES ACROSS					
	GOOD	ADEQ	POOR	BAD	VBAD	TOTAL
PRIV	1.7%	33.9%	22.0%	20.3%	22.0%	59
	1	20	13	12	13	
NCO	0.0%	36.7%	20.0%	23.3%	20.0%	30
	0	11	6	7	6	
WAR	*	*	*	*	*	3
	0	2	0	0	1	
OFF	5.0%	45.0%	10.0%	20.0%	20.0%	20
	1	9	2	4	4	
TOTAL	1.8%	37.5%	18.7%	20.5%	21.4%	112
	2	42	21	23	24	

Exclusion analysis:
Table total: 112
Excluded: 1
Sample size: 113

Table 160

Perceptions By Rank of Unit Effectiveness

64:"In your opinion, how well do you think your unit
would have fought in actual combat"

RANK BY FIGHT

DOWN: Highest rank
ACROSS: How good unit in combat

PERCENTAGES ACROSS

	VWELL	FAIR	MDTLY	POOR	VPOOR	TOTAL
PRIV	8. 8%	31. 6%	33. 3%	22. 8%	3. 5%	57
	5	18	19	13	2	
NCO	11. 5%	46. 2%	38. 5%	3. 8%	0. 0%	26
	3	12	10	1	0	
WAR	*	*	*	*	*	3
	0	2	1	0	0	
OFF	10. 0%	45. 0%	35. 0%	10. 0%	0. 0%	20
	2	9	7	2	0	
TOTAL	9. 4%	38. 7%	34. 9%	15. 1%	1. 9%	106
	10	41	37	16	2	

Exclusion analysis:
Table total: 106
Excluded: 7
Sample size: 113

Table 161

Perceptions By Rank Of The Value Of Ideology As A Motivator
Of Troops

82: "In your opinion, how important do you think that
belief in an ideology -- Marxism- Leninism -- is in
motivating a soldier to fight well"

RANK BY IDEOL

DOWN: Highest rank
ACROSS: Ideology as motivator

PERCENTAGES ACROSS

	MOST	VERY	NOTIMP	UNIMP	TOTAL
PRIV	11. 9%	8. 5%	16. 9%	62. 7%	59
	7	5	10	37	
NCO	10. 0%	10. 0%	20. 0%	60. 0%	30
	3	3	6	18	
WAR	*	*	*	*	3
	0	0	0	3	
OFF	0. 0%	16. 7%	16. 7%	66. 7%	18
	0	3	3	12	
TOTAL	9. 1%	10. 0%	17. 3%	63. 6%	110
	10	11	19	70	

Exclusion analysis:
Table total: 110
Excluded: 3
Sample size: 113

Table 162

Perceptions By Rank Of Factors Motivating Soldiers To Fight Well

83: "Which of the following things do you think is most important to motivating a soldier to fight well?

RANK BY MOTIV

DOWN: Highest rank
ACROSS: Factors motivating sold

PERCENTAGES ACROSS

	TIES	HOME	CARE	IDEO	NOCOW	TOTAL
PRIV	19.3%	14.0%	5.3%	14.0%	47.4%	57
	11	8	3	8	27	
NCO	31.0%	17.2%	0.0%	10.3%	41.4%	29
	9	5	0	3	12	
WAR	*	*	*	*	*	3
	0	1	0	0	2	
OFF	15.8%	26.3%	10.5%	5.3%	42.1%	19
	3	5	2	1	8	
TOTAL	21.3%	17.6%	4.6%	11.1%	45.4%	108
	23	19	5	12	49	

Exclusion analysis:
Table total: 108
Excluded: 5
Sample size: 113

Table 163

Perceptions By Rank Of Officer Quality

98: "Given the general quality of officers that you
served with in your military service, how would you rate
their quality as officers"

RANK BY OFQUAL

DOWN: Highest rank
ACROSS: Officer quality

PERCENTAGES ACROSS
============ ======

	EXGOOD	GOOD	AVG	FAIR	POOR	VPOOR	TOTAL
PRIV	0. 0%	6. 8%	59. 3%	16. 9%	15. 3%	1. 7%	59
	0	4	35	10	9	1	
NCO	0. 0%	13. 8%	58. 6%	6. 9%	20. 7%	0. 0%	29
	0	4	17	2	6	0	
WAR	*	*	*	*	*	*	3
	0	1	2	0	0	0	
OFF	5. 3%	10. 5%	52. 6%	21. 1%	10. 5%	0. 0%	19
	1	2	10	4	2	0	
TOTAL	0. 9%	10. 0%	58. 2%	14. 5%	15. 5%	0. 9%	110
	1	11	64	16	17	1	

Exclusion analysis:
Table total: 110
Excluded: 3
Sample size: 113

Table 164

Perceptions By Rank Of Non-Commissioned Officer Quality

99: "How would you rate the quality of the non-commissione
officers you came in contact with"

RANK BY NCOQUAL

DOWN: Highest rank
ACROSS: NCO quality

PERCENTAGES ACROSS
=========== ======

	EXGOOD	GOOD	AVG	FAIR	POOR	VPOOR	TOTA
PRIV	1.7%	18.6%	44.1%	18.6%	11.9%	5.1%	
	1	11	26	11	7	3	
NCO	0.0%	17.2%	51.7%	20.7%	10.3%	0.0%	
	0	5	15	6	3	0	
WAR	*	*	*	*	*	*	
	0	1	2	0	0	0	
OFF	5.3%	21.1%	36.8%	31.6%	0.0%	5.3%	
	1	4	7	6	0	1	
1							
TOTAL	1.8%	19.1%	45.5%	20.9%	9.1%	3.6%	

Table 165

Perceptions By Rank Of Leadership Elements
Seen in Terms of # 100

**"How Close To Your Fellow Soldiers Did You Feel When
You Were In The Military"**

RANK BY CLOFEL

DOWN: Highest rank
ACROSS: Close with comrades

PERCENTAGES ACROSS

	VCLOSE	CLOSE	MCLOSE	NCLOSE	FEW	TOTAL
PRIV	6.8%	11.9%	25.4%	25.4%	30.5%	59
	4	7	15	15	18	
NCO	3.4%	27.6%	31.0%	6.9%	31.0%	29
	1	8	9	2	9	
WAR	*	*	*	*	*	3
	0	0	3	0	0	
OFF	5.3%	5.3%	31.6%	21.1%	36.8%	19
	1	1	6	4	7	
TOTAL	5.5%	14.5%	30.0%	19.1%	30.9%	110
	6	16	33	21	34	

Exclusion analysis:
Table total: 110
Excluded: 3
Sample size: 113

Table 166

Perceptions By Rank Of Leadership Elements
Seen in Terms of # 101

"How Strongly Did You Develop Feelings Of Pride And
Affection For Your Military Unit"

RANK BY PRIDE

DOWN: Highest rank
ACROSS: Pride in military unit

PERCENTAGES ACROSS
============= ======

	VSTR	STRONG	MDIY	NVSTR	NCON	NPRIDE	TOT
PRIV	1.7%	3.4%	3.4%	27.1%	25.4%	39.0%	
	1	2	2	16	15	23	
NCO	0.0%	3.4%	13.8%	31.0%	17.2%	34.5%	
	0	1	4	9	5	10	
WAR	*	*	*	*	*	*	
	0	0	0	2	0	1	
OFF	5.3%	10.5%	15.8%	5.3%	26.3%	36.8%	
	1	2	3	1	5	7	
TOTAL	1.8%	4.5%	8.2%	25.5%	22.7%	37.3%	
	2	5	9	28	25	41	

Exclusion analysis:
Table total: 110
Excluded: 3
Sample size: 113

Table 167

Perceptions By Rank Of AWOL As a Major Problem

111: "In general, is going absent without leave a big
problem in the military"

RANK BY PROBA

DOWN: Highest rank
ACROSS: AWOL a big problem

PERCENTAGES ACROSS
=========== ======

	YES	NO	TOTAL
PRIV	82.5%	17.5%	57
	47	10	
NCO	85.2%	14.8%	27
	23	4	
WAR	*	*	3
	1	2	
OFF	78.9%	21.1%	19
	15	4	
TOTAL	81.1%	18.9%	106
	86	20	

Exclusion analysis:
Table total: 106
Excluded: 7
Sample size: 113

Table 168

Perceptions By Rank of Desertion As a Major Problem

112: "Is desertion a big problem in the military"

RANK BY PROBD

DOWN: Highest rank
ACROSS: Desertion a big problem

PERCENTAGES ACROSS

	YES	NO	TOTAL
PRIV	50. 0%	50. 0%	56
	28	28	
NCO	65. 4%	34. 6%	26
	17	9	
WAR	*	*	3
	1	2	
OFF	42. 1%	57. 9%	19
	8	11	
TOTAL	51. 9%	48. 1%	104
	54	50	

Exclusion analysis:
Table total: 104
Excluded: 9
Sample size: 113

Table 169

Perceptions By Rank Of Leadership Elements
Seen in Terms of # 116

**"Seemed More Concerned With His Own Career Advancement
Than With His Men"**

RANK BY CARADV

DOWN: Highest rank
ACROSS: Career advancement

PERCENTAGES ACROSS

	OFF	NCO	WAR	ALL	TOTAL
PRIV	28. 8%	11. 5%	11. 5%	48. 1%	52
	15	6	6	25	
NCO	35. 7%	17. 9%	0. 0%	46. 4%	28
	10	5	0	13	
WAR	*	*	*	*	3
	3	0	0	0	
OFF	60. 0%	0. 0%	0. 0%	40. 0%	15
	9	0	0	6	
TOTAL	37. 8%	11. 2%	6. 1%	44. 9%	98
	37	11	6	44	

Exclusion analysis:
Table total: 98
Excluded: 15
Sample size: 113

Table 170

Perceptions By Rank Of Leadership Elements
Seen in Terms of # 120

"Shared Hardships With His Troops"

RANK BY HARSHP

DOWN: Highest rank
ACROSS: Shared hardship with men

PERCENTAGES ACROSS
========== ======

	OFF	NCO	WAR	ALL	TOTAL
PRIV	3. 7%	51. 9%	11. 1%	33. 3%	27
	1	14	3	9	
NCO	14. 3%	64. 3%	0. 0%	21. 4%	14
	2	9	0	3	
WAR	*	*	*	*	1
	0	0	1	0	
OFF	30. 8%	15. 4%	7. 7%	46. 2%	13
	4	2	1	6	
TOTAL	12. 7%	45. 5%	9. 1%	32. 7%	55
	7	25	5	18	

Exclusion analysis:
Table total: 55
Excluded: 58
Sample size: 113

Table 171

Perceptions By Rank Of Leadership Elements
Seen in Terms of # 128

"Often Tried To Avoid Taking Responsibility When
Things Went Wrong"

RANK BY WRONG

DOWN: Highest rank
ACROSS: Avoided responsibility

PERCENTAGES ACROSS

	OFF	NCO	WAR	ALL	TOTAL
PRIV	14. 9%	14. 9%	6. 4%	63. 8%	47
	7	7	3	30	
NCO	16. 7%	25. 0%	8. 3%	50. 0%	24
	4	6	2	12	
WAR	*	*	*	*	2
	1	1	0	0	
OFF	50. 0%	0. 0%	0. 0%	50. 0%	12
	6	0	0	6	
TOTAL	21. 2%	16. 5%	5. 9%	56. 5%	85
	18	14	5	48	

Exclusion analysis:
Table total: 85
Excluded: 28
Sample size: 113

Table 172

Perceptions By Rank Of Leadership Elements
Seen in Terms of # 126

"Never Developed Close Personal Ties With His Men"

RANK BY NOPETI

DOWN: Highest rank
ACROSS: No personal ties

PERCENTAGES ACROSS

	OFF	NCO	WAR	ALL	TOTAL
PRIV	33. 3%	11. 1%	11. 1%	44. 4%	36
	12	4	4	16	
NCO	37. 5%	12. 5%	0. 0%	50. 0%	16
	6	2	0	8	
WAR	*	*	*	*	1
	1	0	0	0	
OFF	58. 3%	0. 0%	0. 0%	41. 7%	12
	7	0	0	5	
TOTAL	40. 0%	9. 2%	6. 2%	44. 6%	65
	26	6	4	29	

Exclusion analysis:
Table total: 65
Excluded: 48
Sample size: 113

Table 173

Perceptions By Rank Of Leadership Elements
Seen in Terms of # 131

"Would Make A Good Man To Go Into Combat With"

RANK BY COMGUD

DOWN: Highest rank
ACROSS: Good man in combat

PERCENTAGES ACROSS

	OFF	NCO	WAR	ALL	TOTAL
PRIV	46.7%	46.7%	0.0%	6.7%	15
	7	7	0	1	
NCO	50.0%	25.0%	16.7%	8.3%	12
	6	3	2	1	
WAR	*	*	*	*	2
	1	1	0	0	
OFF	55.6%	33.3%	0.0%	11.1%	9
	5	3	0	1	
TOTAL	50.0%	36.8%	5.3%	7.9%	38
	19	14	2	3	

Exclusion analysis:
Table total: 38
Excluded: 75
Sample size: 113

Table 174

Perceptions By Rank Of Leadership Elements
Seen in Terms of # 136

"Used His Position To Take Advantage Of Other Soldiers"

RANK BY USEPO

DOWN: Highest rank
ACROSS: Used position/take advantage

PERCENTAGES ACROSS
========== ======

	OFF	NCO	WAR	ALL	TOTAL
PRIV	17.0%	14.9%	14.9%	53.2%	47
	8	7	7	25	
NCO	19.0%	9.5%	14.3%	57.1%	21
	4	2	3	12	
WAR	*	*	*	*	3
	1	0	1	1	
OFF	9.1%	9.1%	9.1%	72.7%	11
	1	1	1	8	
TOTAL	17.1%	12.2%	14.6%	56.1%	82
	14	10	12	46	

Exclusion analysis:
Table total: 82
Excluded: 31
Sample size: 113

Table 175

Perceptions By Rank Of Leadership Elements
Seen in Terms of # 141

"Tended To Limit His Contact With His Men"

RANK BY LIMCON

DOWN: Highest rank
ACROSS: Limit contact with men

PERCENTAGES ACROSS

	OFF	NCO	WAR	ALL	TOTAL
PRIV	48.6%	8.1%	2.7%	40.5%	37
	18	3	1	15	
NCO	47.4%	15.8%	0.0%	36.8%	19
	9	3	0	7	
WAR	*	*	*	*	2
	1	0	1	0	
OFF	63.6%	0.0%	9.1%	27.3%	11
	7	0	1	3	
TOTAL	50.7%	8.7%	4.3%	36.2%	69
	35	6	3	25	

Exclusion analysis:
Table total: 69
Excluded: 44
Sample size: 113

Table 176

Perceptions By Rank Of Leadership Elements
Seen in Terms of # 143

"He Was A Good Example To Young Soldiers"

RANK BY GOODEX

DOWN: Highest rank
ACROSS: Good example for men

PERCENTAGES ACROSS

	OFF	NCO	WAR	ALL	TOTAL
PRIV	25. 0%	50. 0%	10. 0%	15. 0%	20
	5	10	2	3	
NCO	23. 1%	23. 1%	7. 7%	46. 2%	13
	3	3	1	6	
WAR	*	*	*	*	2
	0	1	1	0	
OFF	75. 0%	25. 0%	0. 0%	0. 0%	8

Table 177

Perceptions By Rank Of Leadership Elements
Seen in Terms of # 146

"Tended To Blame Others For Things He Was Supposed To Do
When They Went Wrong"

RANK BY BLAME

DOWN: Highest rank
ACROSS: Blame others for errors

PERCENTAGES ACROSS

	OFF	NCO	WAR	ALL	TOTAL
PRIV	14.3%	11.9%	9.5%	64.3%	42
	6	5	4	27	
NCO	10.0%	25.0%	10.0%	55.0%	20
	2	5	2	11	
WAR	*	*	*	*	3
	0	0	2	1	
OFF	22.2%	11.1%	11.1%	55.6%	9
	2	1	1	5	
TOTAL	13.5%	14.9%	12.2%	59.5%	74
	10	11	9	44	

Exclusion analysis:
Table total: 74
Excluded: 39
Sample size: 113

Table 178

Perceptions Of The Combat Ability Of Soviet Units By Rank

151: "On a scale of from 1 to 10 in which 1 is the worst and 10 is the best, how well do you think your unit would so in actual combat"

RANK BY SCALCO

DOWN: Highest rank
ACROSS: Scale of combat ability

PERCENTAGES ACROSS

	1	2	3	4	5	6	7	8	9	10	TOTAL
PRIV	5.5% 3	3.6% 2	27.3% 15	14.5% 8	12.7% 7	9.1% 5	16.4% 9	5.5% 3	1.8% 1	3.6% 2	55
NCO	0.0% 0	0.0% 0	3.4% 1	13.8% 4	20.7% 6	20.7% 6	13.8% 4	17.2% 5	0.0% 0	10.3% 3	29
WAR	* 0	* 0	* 0	* 1	* 1	* 0	* 0	* 1	* 0	* 0	3
OFF	0.0% 0	0.0% 0	10.5% 2	15.8% 3	15.8% 3	10.5% 2	15.8% 3	21.1% 4	5.3% 1	5.3% 1	19
TOTAL	2.8% 3	1.9% 2	17.0% 18	15.1% 16	16.0% 17	12.3% 13	15.1% 16	12.3% 13	1.9% 2	5.7% 6	106

Exclusion analysis:
Table total: 106
Excluded: 7
Sample size: 113

Table 179

Perceptions Of The Quality of Soviet Training By Rank

#156: "On a scale of from 1 to 10 in which 1 is the worst and 10 is the best, how would you rate the military training your unit received"

RANK BY TRAIN

DOWN: Highest rank
ACROSS: Quality of training

PERCENTAGES ACROSS
=================

	1	2	3	4	5	6	7	8	9	10	TOTAL
PRIV	8.9% 5	10.7% 6	16.1% 9	7.1% 4	23.2% 13	5.4% 3	14.3% 8	7.1% 4	3.6% 2	3.6% 2	56
NCO	0.0% 0	6.9% 2	6.9% 2	0.0% 0	13.8% 4	13.8% 4	13.8% 4	31.0% 9	3.4% 1	10.3% 3	29
WAR	* 	* 	* 	* 	* 1	* 	* 2	* 	* 	* 	3
OFF	0.0% 0	0.0% 0	15.8% 3	26.3% 5	10.5% 2	0.0% 0	21.1% 4	15.8% 3	0.0% 0	10.5% 2	19
TOTAL	4.7% 5	7.5% 8	13.1% 14	8.4% 9	18.7% 20	6.5% 7	16.8% 18	15.0% 16	2.8% 3	6.5% 7	107

Exclusion analysis:
Table total: 107
Excluded: 6
Sample size: 113

Table 180

Perceptions of Combat Ability of Soviet Units
By Commanders By Mean Score Of A
Maximum Scale Score of 10

Position	N	Mean Score
Enlisted Commanders	17	2.8
Enlisted Supervisors	16	2.3
Officer Commanders	12	2.9
Officer Supervisors	8	1.6
Troops	55	2.9

Table 181

Commanders Perceptions of the Quality
Of Soviet Military Training By Mean Score
Of A Maximum Scale Score of 10

Position	N	Mean Score
Enlisted Commanders	17	5.6
Enlisted Supervisors	16	6.8
Officer Commanders	12	6.8
Officer Supervisors	8	4.6
Troops	54	4.9

Table 182

How Enlisted Commanders (COMEN), Enlisted Supervisors
(SUPEN), Officer Commanders (COMOFF), Supervisory Of-
ficers (SUPOFF) and Those Holding No Position (NONE)
Perceived Leadership Elements Relative To Question # 64

"In your opinion, how well do you think your unit would
have fought in actual combat"

RANTI BY FIGHT

DOWN: Rank title
ACROSS: How good unit in combat

PERCENTAGES ACROSS

	VWELL	FAIR	MDTLY	POOR	VPOOR	TOTAL
COMEN	6.2%	37.5%	50.0%	6.2%	0.0%	16
	1	6	8	1	0	
SUPEN	13.3%	53.3%	33.3%	0.0%	0.0%	15
	2	8	5	0	0	
COMOFF	16.7%	41.7%	41.7%	0.0%	0.0%	12
	2	5	5	0	0	
SUPOFF	0.0%	55.6%	33.3%	11.1%	0.0%	9
	0	5	3	1	0	
NONE	9.3%	31.5%	29.6%	25.9%	3.7%	54
	5	17	16	14	2	
TOTAL	9.4%	38.7%	34.9%	15.1%	1.9%	106
	10	41	37	16	2	

Exclusion analysis:
Table total: 106
Excluded: 7
Sample size: 113

Table 183

How Enlisted Commanders (COMEN), Enlisted Supervisors (SUPEN), Officer Commanders (COMOFF), Supervisory Officers (SUPOFF) and Those Holding No Position (NONE) Perceived Leadership Elements Relative To Question # 82

"In your opinion, how important do you think that belief in an ideology -- Marxism- Leninism -- is in motivating a soldier to fight well"

RANTI BY IDEOL

DOWN: Rank title
ACROSS: Ideology as motivator

PERCENTAGES ACROSS

	MOST	VERY	NOTIMP	UNIMP	TOTAL
COMEN	16. 7%	11. 1%	11. 1%	61. 1%	18
	3	2	2	11	
SUPEN	6. 2%	6. 2%	25. 0%	62. 5%	16
	1	1	4	10	
COMOFF	0. 0%	16. 7%	16. 7%	66. 7%	12
	0	2	2	8	
SUPOFF	0. 0%	14. 3%	14. 3%	71. 4%	7
	0	1	1	5	
NONE	10. 5%	8. 8%	17. 5%	63. 2%	57
	6	5	10	36	
TOTAL	9. 1%	10. 0%	17. 3%	63. 6%	110
	10	11	19	70	

Exclusion analysis:
Table total: 110
Excluded: 3
Sample size: 113

Table 184

How Enlisted Commanders (COMEN), Enlisted Supervisors
(SUPEN), Officer Commanders (COMOFF), Supervisory Of-
ficers (SUPOFF) and Those Holding No Position (NONE)
Perceived Leadership Elements Relative To Question # 83

"Which of the following things do you think is most
important to motivating a soldier to fight well"

RANTI BY MOTIV

DOWN: Rank title
ACROSS: Factors motivating sold

PERCENTAGES ACROSS

	TIES	HOME	CARE	IDEO	NOCOW	TOTAL
COMEN	35. 3%	23. 5%	0. 0%	11. 8%	29. 4%	17
	6	4	0	2	5	
SUPEN	26. 7%	13. 3%	0. 0%	13. 3%	46. 7%	15
	4	2	0	2	7	
COMOFF	0. 0%	25. 0%	16. 7%	8. 3%	50. 0%	12
	0	3	2	1	6	
SUPOFF	37. 5%	37. 5%	0. 0%	0. 0%	25. 0%	8
	3	3	0	0	2	
NONE	17. 9%	12. 5%	5. 4%	12. 5%	51. 8%	56
	10	7	3	7	29	
TOTAL	21. 3%	17. 6%	4. 6%	11. 1%	45. 4%	108
	23	19	5	12	49	

Exclusion analysis:
Table total: 108
Excluded: 5
Sample size: 113

Table 185

How Enlisted Commanders (COMEN), Enlisted Supervisors
(SUPEN), Officer Commanders (COMOFF), Supervisory Of-
ficers (SUPOFF) and Those Holding No Position (NONE)
Perceived Leadership Elements Relative To Question # 98

"Given the general quality of officers that you served
with in your military service, how would you rate their
quality as officers"

RANTI BY OFQUAL

DOWN: Rank title
ACROSS: Officer quality

PERCENTAGES ACROSS

	EXGOOD	GOOD	AVG	FAIR	POOR	VPOOR	TOTAL
COMEN	0. 0%	11. 8%	58. 8%	5. 9%	23. 5%	0. 0%	17
	0	2	10	1	4	0	
SUPEN	0. 0%	18. 7%	56. 2%	12. 5%	12. 5%	0. 0%	16
	0	3	9	2	2	0	
COMOFF	8. 3%	8. 3%	66. 7%	16. 7%	0. 0%	0. 0%	12
	1	1	8	2	0	0	
SUPOFF	0. 0%	12. 5%	50. 0%	25. 0%	12. 5%	0. 0%	8
	0	1	4	2	1	0	
NONE	0. 0%	7. 0%	57. 9%	15. 8%	17. 5%	1. 8%	57
	0	4	33	9	10	1	
TOTAL	0. 9%	10. 0%	58. 2%	14. 5%	15. 5%	0. 9%	110
	1	11	64	16	17	1	

Exclusion analysis:
Table total: 110
Excluded: 3
Sample size: 113

Table 186

How Enlisted Commanders (COMEN), Enlisted Supervisors (SUPEN), Officer Commanders (COMOFF), Supervisory Officers (SUPOFF) and Those Holding No Position (NONE) Perceived Leadership Elements Relative To Question # 99

"How would you rate the quality of the non-commissioned officers you came into contact with"

RANTI BY NCOQUAL

DOWN: Rank title
ACROSS: NCO quality

PERCENTAGES ACROSS

	EXGOOD	GOOD	AVG	FAIR	POOR	VPOOR	TOTAL
COMEN	0. 0%	17. 6%	52. 9%	23. 5%	5. 9%	0. 0%	17
	0	3	9	4	1	0	
SUPEN	0. 0%	25. 0%	37. 5%	37. 5%	0. 0%	0. 0%	16
	0	4	6	6	0	0	
COMOFF	8. 3%	33. 3%	33. 3%	16. 7%	0. 0%	8. 3%	12
	1	4	4	2	0	1	
SUPOFF	0. 0%	0. 0%	50. 0%	50. 0%	0. 0%	0. 0%	8
	0	0	4	4	0	0	
NONE	1. 8%	17. 5%	47. 4%	12. 3%	15. 8%	5. 3%	57
	1	10	27	7	9	3	
TOTAL	1. 8%	19. 1%	45. 5%	20. 9%	9. 1%	3. 6%	110
	2	21	50	23	10	4	

Exclusion analysis:
Table total: 110
Excluded: 3
Sample size: 113

Table 187

How Enlisted Commanders (COMEN), Enlisted Supervisors
(SUPEN), Officer Commanders (COMOFF), Supervisory Of-
ficers (SUPOFF) and Those Holding No Position (NONE)
Perceived Leadership Elements Relative To Question # 100

"How close to your fellow soldiers did you feel when
you were in the military"

RANTI BY CLOFEL

DOWN: Rank title
ACROSS: Close with comrades

PERCENTAGES ACROSS

	VCLOSE	CLOSE	MCLOSE	NCLOSE	FEW	TOTAL
COMEN	0. 0%	41. 2%	23. 5%	5. 9%	29. 4%	17
	0	7	4	1	5	
SUPEN	6. 2%	12. 5%	50. 0%	12. 5%	18. 7%	16
	1	2	8	2	3	
COMOFF	8. 3%	0. 0%	50. 0%	8. 3%	33. 3%	12
	1	0	6	1	4	
SUPOFF	0. 0%	0. 0%	25. 0%	37. 5%	37. 5%	8
	0	0	2	3	3	
NONE	7. 0%	12. 3%	22. 8%	24. 6%	33. 3%	57
	4	7	13	14	19	
TOTAL	5. 5%	14. 5%	30. 0%	19. 1%	30. 9%	110
	6	16	33	21	34	

Exclusion analysis:
Table total: 110
Excluded: 3
Sample size: 113

Table 188

How Enlisted Commanders, (COMEN), Enlisted Supervisors
(SUPEN), Officer Commanders (COMOFF), Supervisory Of-
ficers (SUPOFF) and Those Holding No Position (NONE)
Perceived Leadership Elements Relative To Question # 111

"In general, is going absent without leave a big problem
in the military"

RANTI BY PROBA

DOWN: Rank title
ACROSS: AWOL a big problem

PERCENTAGES ACROSS

	YES	NO	TOTAL
COMEN	88.2%	11.8%	17
	15	2	
SUPEN	78.6%	21.4%	14
	11	3	
COMOFF	63.6%	36.4%	11
	7	4	
SUPOFF	88.9%	11.1%	9
	8	1	
NONE	81.8%	18.2%	55
	45	10	
TOTAL	81.1%	18.9%	106
	86	20	

Exclusion analysis:
Table total: 106
Excluded: 7
Sample size: 113

Table 189

How Enlisted Commanders (COMEN), Enlisted Supervisors
(SUPEN), Officer Commanders (COMOFF), Supervisory Of-
ficers (SUPOFF) and Those Holding No Position (NONE)
Perceived Leadership Elements Relative To Question # 112

"Is desertion a big problem in the military"

RANTI BY PROBD

DOWN: Rank title
ACROSS: Desertion a big problem

PERCENTAGES ACROSS

	YES	NO	TOTAL
COMEN	80.0%	20.0%	15
	12	3	
SUPEN	40.0%	60.0%	15
	6	9	
COMOFF	36.4%	63.6%	11
	4	7	
SUPOFF	44.4%	55.6%	9
	4	5	
NONE	51.9%	48.1%	54
	28	26	
TOTAL	51.9%	48.1%	104
	54	50	

Exclusion analysis:
Table total: 104
Excluded: 9
Sample size: 113

Table 190

How Enlisted Commanders (COMEN), Enlisted Supervisors (SUPEN), Officer Commanders (COMOFF), Supervisory Officers (SUPOFF) and Those Holding No Position (NONE) Perceived Leadership Elements Relative To Question # 116

"Seemed more concerned with his own career advancement than with his men"

RANTI BY CARADV

DOWN: Rank title
ACROSS: Career advancement

PERCENTAGES ACROSS

	OFF	NCO	WAR	ALL	TOTAL
COMEN	23.5%	23.5%	0.0%	52.9%	17
	4	4	0	9	
SUPEN	37.5%	18.7%	0.0%	43.7%	16
	6	3	0	7	
COMOFF	70.0%	0.0%	0.0%	30.0%	10
	7	0	0	3	
SUPOFF	66.7%	0.0%	0.0%	33.3%	6
	4	0	0	2	
NONE	32.7%	8.2%	12.2%	46.9%	49
	16	4	6	23	
TOTAL	37.8%	11.2%	6.1%	44.9%	98
	37	11	6	44	

Exclusion analysis:
Table total: 98
Excluded: 15
Sample size: 113

Table 191

How Enlisted Commanders (COMEN), Enlisted Supervisors (SUPEN),Officer Commanders (COMOFF), Supervisory Officers (SUPOFF) and Those Holding No Position (NONE) Perceived Leadership Elements Relative To Question # 117

"He treated people in an impersonal manner - - like cogs in a machine"

RANTI BY COGS

DOWN: Rank title
ACROSS: Treated men impersonally

PERCENTAGES ACROSS

	OFF	NCO	WAR	ALL	TOTAL
COMEN	20. 0%	13. 3%	6. 7%	60. 0%	15
	3	2	1	9	
SUPEN	42. 9%	21. 4%	7. 1%	28. 6%	14
	6	3	1	4	
COMOFF	37. 5%	12. 5%	12. 5%	37. 5%	8
	3	1	1	3	
SUPOFF	42. 9%	0. 0%	14. 3%	42. 9%	7
	3	0	1	3	
NONE	35. 7%	4. 8%	7. 1%	52. 4%	42
	15	2	3	22	
TOTAL	34. 9%	9. 3%	8. 1%	47. 7%	86
	30	8	7	41	

Exclusion analysis:
Table total: 86
Excluded: 27
Sample size: 113

Table 192

How Enlisted Commanders (COMEN), Enlisted Supervisors (SUPEN), Officer Commanders (COMOFF), Supervisory Officers (SUPOFF) and Those Holding No Position (NONE) Perceived Leadership Elements Relative To Question # 120

"Shared hardships with his troops"

RANTI BY HARSHP

DOWN: Rank title
ACROSS: Shared hardship with men

PERCENTAGES ACROSS

	OFF	NCO	WAR	ALL	TOTAL
COMEN	*	*	*	*	4
	1	0	0	3	
SUPEN	7.7%	84.6%	0.0%	7.7%	13
	1	11	0	1	
COMOFF	27.3%	18.2%	9.1%	45.5%	11
	3	2	1	5	
SUPOFF	*	*	*	*	3
	1	0	1	1	
NONE	4.2%	50.0%	12.5%	33.3%	24
	1	12	3	8	
TOTAL	12.7%	45.5%	9.1%	32.7%	55
	7	25	5	18	

Exclusion analysis:
Table total: 55
Excluded: 58
Sample size: 113

Table 193

How Enlisted Commanders (COMEN), Enlisted Supervisors
(SUPEN), Officer Commanders (COMOFF), Supervisory Of-
ficers (SUPOFF) and Those Holding No Position (NONE)
Perceived Leadership Elements Relative To Question # 123

"Drew too strong a line between himself and his men;
he was too distant"

RANTI BY DIST

DOWN: Rank title
ACROSS: Was too distant

PERCENTAGES ACROSS

	OFF	NCO	WAR	ALL	TOTAL
COMEN	46. 7%	6. 7%	6. 7%	40. 0%	15
	7	1	1	6	
SUPEN	36. 4%	27. 3%	9. 1%	27. 3%	11
	4	3	1	3	
COMOFF	90. 0%	0. 0%	10. 0%	0. 0%	10
	9	0	1	0	
SUPOFF	50. 0%	0. 0%	0. 0%	50. 0%	6
	3	0	0	3	
NONE	40. 9%	9. 1%	9. 1%	40. 9%	44
	18	4	4	18	
TOTAL	47. 7%	9. 3%	8. 1%	34. 9%	86
	41	8	7	30	

Exclusion analysis:
Table total: 86
Excluded: 27
Sample size: 113

Table 194

How Enlisted Commanders (COMEN), Enlisted Supervisors
(SUPEN), Officer Commanders (COMOFF), Supervisory Of-
ficers (SUPOFF) and Those Holding No Position (NONE)
Perceived Leadership Elements Relative To Question # 124

"Had the kind of judgement I would trust in combat"

RANTI BY JUDGE

DOWN: Rank title
ACROSS: Had judgement/combat

PERCENTAGES ACROSS
========== ======

	OFF	NCO	WAR	ALL	TOTAL
COMEN	50. 0%	33. 3%	0. 0%	16. 7%	6
	3	2	0	1	
SUPEN	*	*	*	*	5
	3	1	0	1	
COMOFF	62. 5%	25. 0%	0. 0%	12. 5%	8
	5	2	0	1	
SUPOFF	*	*	*	*	1
	1	0	0	0	
NONE	50. 0%	22. 2%	5. 6%	22. 2%	18
	9	4	1	4	
TOTAL	55. 3%	23. 7%	2. 6%	18. 4%	38
	21	9	1	7	

Exclusion analysis:
Table total: 38
Excluded: 75
Sample size: 113

Table 195

How Enlisted Commanders (COMEN), Enlisted Supervisors
(SUPEN), Officer Commanders (COMOFF), Supervisory Of-
ficers (SUPOFF), and Those Holding No Position (NONE)
Perceived Leadership Elements Relative To Question # 126

"Never developed close personal ties with his men"

RANTI BY NOPETI

DOWN: Rank title
ACROSS: No personal ties

PERCENTAGES ACROSS

	OFF	NCO	WAR	ALL		TOTAL
COMEN	37. 5%	0. 0%	0. 0%	62. 5%		8
	3	0	0	5		
SUPEN	20. 0%	10. 0%	0. 0%	70. 0%		10
	2	1	0	7		
COMOFF	70. 0%	0. 0%	0. 0%	30. 0%		10
	7	0	0	3		
SUPOFF	*	*	*	*		3
	1	0	0	2		
NONE	38. 2%	14. 7%	11. 8%	35. 3%		34
	13	5	4	12		
TOTAL	40. 0%	9. 2%	6. 2%	44. 6%		65
	26	6	4	29		

Exclusion analysis:
Table total: 65
Excluded: 48
Sample size: 113

Table 196

How Enlisted Commanders (COMEN), Enlisted Supervisors
(SUPEN), Officer Commanders (COMOFF), Supervisory Of-
ficers (SUPOFF) and Those Holding No Position (NONE)
Perceived Leadership Elements Relative To Question # 128

"Often tried to avoid taking responsiblity when
things went wrong"

RANTI BY WRONG

DOWN: Rank title
ACROSS: Avoided responsibility

PERCENTAGES ACROSS

	OFF	NCO	WAR	ALL	TOTAL
COMEN	20. 0%	6. 7%	6. 7%	66. 7%	15
	3	1	1	10	
SUPEN	8. 3%	41. 7%	8. 3%	41. 7%	12
	1	5	1	5	
COMOFF	57. 1%	0. 0%	0. 0%	42. 9%	7
	4	0	0	3	
SUPOFF	50. 0%	0. 0%	0. 0%	50. 0%	6
	3	0	0	3	
NONE	15. 6%	17. 8%	6. 7%	60. 0%	45
	7	8	3	27	
TOTAL	21. 2%	16. 5%	5. 9%	56. 5%	85
	18	14	5	48	

Exclusion analysis:
Table total: 85
Excluded: 28
Sample size: 113

Table 197

How Enlisted Commanders (COMEN), Enlisted Supervisors (SUPEN), Officer Commanders (COMOFF), Supervisory Officers (SUPOFF) and Those Holding No position (NONE) Perceived Leadership Elements Relative to Question # 131

"Would make a good man to go into combat with"

RANTI BY COMGUD

DOWN: Rank title
ACROSS: Good man in combat

PERCENTAGES ACROSS

	OFF	NCO	WAR	ALL	TOTAL
COMEN	*	*	*	*	5
	3	1	1	0	
SUPEN	50.0%	16.7%	16.7%	16.7%	6
	3	1	1	1	
COMOFF	60.0%	30.0%	0.0%	10.0%	10
	6	3	0	1	
SUPOFF	*	*	*	*	1
	0	1	0	0	
NONE	43.7%	50.0%	0.0%	6.2%	16
	7	8	0	1	
TOTAL	50.0%	36.8%	5.3%	7.9%	38
	19	14	2	3	

Exclusion analysis:
Table total: 38
Excluded: 75
Sample size: 113

Table 198

How Enlisted Commanders (COMEN), Enlisted Supervisors (SUPEN), Officer Commanders (COMOFF), Supervisory Officers (SUPOFF) and Those Holding No Position (NONE) Perceived Leadership Elements Relative To Question # 132

"He would probably distort reports to make himself look better"

RANTI BY DISTO

DOWN: Rank title
ACROSS: Distort reports/career

PERCENTAGES ACROSS
========== ======

	OFF	NCO	WAR	ALL	TOTAL
COMEN	0.0%	7.1%	21.4%	71.4%	14
	0	1	3	10	
SUPEN	9.1%	45.5%	9.1%	36.4%	11
	1	5	1	4	
COMOFF	42.9%	14.3%	0.0%	42.9%	7
	3	1	0	3	
SUPOFF	*	*	*	*	4
	0	0	1	3	
NONE	18.4%	15.8%	10.5%	55.3%	38
	7	6	4	21	
TOTAL	14.9%	17.6%	12.2%	55.4%	74
	11	13	9	41	

Exclusion analysis:
Table total: 74
Excluded: 39
Sample size: 113

197

Table 199

How Enlisted Commanders (COMEN), Enlisted Supervisors (SUPEN), Officer Commanders (COMOFF), Supervisory Officers (SUPOFF) and Those Holding No Position (NONE) Perceived Leadership Elements Relative to Question # 133

"He was overly ambitious at the expense of his subordinates and his unit"

RANTI BY OVAMB

DOWN: Rank title
ACROSS: Overly ambitious

PERCENTAGES ACROSS

	OFF	NCO	WAR	ALL	TOTAL
COMEN	7. 1%	0. 0%	7. 1%	85. 7%	14
	1	0	1	12	
SUPEN	8. 3%	50. 0%	8. 3%	33. 3%	12
	1	6	1	4	
COMOFF	77. 8%	0. 0%	11. 1%	11. 1%	9
	7	0	1	1	
SUPOFF	*	*	*	*	3
	0	1	0	2	
NONE	28. 2%	7. 7%	17. 9%	46. 2%	39
	11	3	7	18	
TOTAL	26. 0%	13. 0%	13. 0%	48. 1%	77
	20	10	10	37	

Exclusion analysis:
Table total: 77
Excluded: 36
Sample size: 113

Table 200

How Enlisted Commanders (COMEN), Enlisted Supervisors
(SUPEN), Officer Commanders (COMOFF), Supervisory Of-
ficers (SUPOFF), and Those Holding No Position (NONE)
Perceived Leadership Elements Relative To Question # 134

"Tended to concentrate on the small unimportant things"

RANTI BY UNIMP

DOWN: Rank title
ACROSS: Looks at small things

PERCENTAGES ACROSS

	OFF	NCO	WAR	ALL	TOTAL
COMEN	7. 7%	15. 4%	15. 4%	61. 5%	13
	1	2	2	8	
SUPEN	16. 7%	41. 7%	16. 7%	25. 0%	12
	2	5	2	3	
COMOFF	16. 7%	33. 3%	16. 7%	33. 3%	6
	1	2	1	2	
SUPOFF	*	*	*	*	4
	1	0	0	3	
NONE	16. 2%	21. 6%	18. 9%	43. 2%	37
	6	8	7	16	
TOTAL	15. 3%	23. 6%	16. 7%	44. 4%	72
	11	17	12	32	

Exclusion analysis:
Table total: 72
Excluded: 41
Sample size: 113

Table 201

How Enlisted Commanders (COMEN), Enlisted Supervisors
(SUPEN), Officer Commanders (COMOFF), Supervisory Of-
ficers (SUPOFF), and Those Holding No Position (NONE)
Perceived Leadership Elements Relative To Question # 136

"Used his position to take advantage of other soldiers"

RANTI BY USEPO

DOWN: Rank title
ACROSS: Used position/take advantage

PERCENTAGES ACROSS

	OFF	NCO	WAR	ALL	TOTAL
COMEN	13. 3%	0. 0%	6. 7%	80. 0%	15
	2	0	1	12	
SUPEN	18. 2%	27. 3%	18. 2%	36. 4%	11
	2	3	2	4	
COMOFF	25. 0%	12. 5%	12. 5%	50. 0%	8
	2	1	1	4	
SUPOFF	*	*	*	*	4
	0	0	1	3	
NONE	18. 2%	13. 6%	15. 9%	52. 3%	44
	8	6	7	23	
TOTAL	17. 1%	12. 2%	14. 6%	56. 1%	82
	14	10	12	46	

Exclusion analysis:
Table total: 82
Excluded: 31
Sample size: 113

Table 202

How Enlisted Commanders (COMEN), Enlisted Supervisors
(SUPEN), Officer Commanders (COMOFF), Supervisory Of-
ficers (SUPOFF) and Those Holding No Position (NONE)
Perceived Leadership Elements Relative To Question # 137

"Stifled the initiative of others"

RANTI BY STIFLE

DOWN: Rank title
ACROSS: Stifled initiative

PERCENTAGES ACROSS
========== ======

	OFF	NCO	WAR	ALL	TOTAL
COMEN	18. 2%	0. 0%	18. 2%	63. 6%	11
	2	0	2	7	
SUPEN	18. 2%	27. 3%	18. 2%	36. 4%	11
	2	3	2	4	
COMOFF	28. 6%	14. 3%	14. 3%	42. 9%	7
	2	1	1	3	
SUPOFF	*	*	*	*	3
	1	1	0	1	
NONE	17. 9%	17. 9%	10. 7%	53. 6%	28
	5	5	3	15	
TOTAL	20. 0%	16. 7%	13. 3%	50. 0%	60
	12	10	8	30	

Exclusion analysis:
Table total: 60
Excluded: 53
Sample size: 113

Table 203

How Enlisted Commanders (COMEN), Enlisted Supervisors
(SUPEN), Officer Commanders (COMOFF), Supervisory Of-
ficers (SUPOFF) and Those Holding No Position (NONE)
Perceived Leadership Elements Relative to Question # 140

"He would hesitate to take actions in the absence of
instructions from his superiors"

RANTI BY HESIT

DOWN: Rank title
ACROSS: Hesitate to act

PERCENTAGES ACROSS

	OFF	NCO	WAR	ALL	TOTAL
COMEN	0. 0%	7. 7%	23. 1%	69. 2%	13
	0	1	3	9	
SUPEN	20. 0%	10. 0%	10. 0%	60. 0%	10
	2	1	1	6	
COMOFF	25. 0%	12. 5%	25. 0%	37. 5%	8
	2	1	2	3	
SUPOFF	*	*	*	*	5
	1	1	0	3	
NONE	17. 9%	17. 9%	2. 6%	61. 5%	39
	7	7	1	24	
TOTAL	16. 0%	14. 7%	9. 3%	60. 0%	75
	12	11	7	45	

Exclusion analysis:
Table total: 75
Excluded: 38
Sample size: 113

Table 204

How Enlisted Commanders (COMEN), Enlisted Supervisors
(SUPEN), Officer Commanders (COMOFF), Supervisory Of-
ficers (SUPOFF) and Those Holding No Position (NONE)
Perceived Leadership Elements Relative To Question # 143

"He was a good example to young soldiers"

RANTI BY GOODEX

DOWN: Rank title
ACROSS: Good example for men

PERCENTAGES ACROSS

	OFF	NCO	WAR	ALL	TOTAL
COMEN	25.0%	37.5%	12.5%	25.0%	8
	2	3	1	2	
SUPEN	20.0%	30.0%	10.0%	40.0%	10
	2	3	1	4	
COMOFF	71.4%	14.3%	14.3%	0.0%	7
	5	1	1	0	
SUPOFF	*	*	*	*	2
	1	1	0	0	
NONE	25.0%	50.0%	6.2%	18.7%	16
	4	8	1	3	
TOTAL	32.6%	37.2%	9.3%	20.9%	43
	14	16	4	9	

Exclusion analysis:
Table total: 43
Excluded: 70
Sample size: 113

Table 205

How Enlisted Commanders (COMEN), Enlisted Supervisors
(SUPEN), Officer Commanders (COMOFF), Supervisory Of-
ficers (SUPOFF) and Those Holding No Position (NONE)
Perceived Leadership Elements Relative To Question # 145

"He was selfish"

RANTI BY SELF

DOWN: Rank title
ACROSS: Selfish person

PERCENTAGES ACROSS
=========== ======

	OFF	NCO	WAR	ALL	TOTAL
COMEN	0. 0%	15. 4%	7. 7%	76. 9%	13
	0	2	1	10	
SUPEN	16. 7%	25. 0%	16. 7%	41. 7%	12
	2	3	2	5	
COMOFF	*	*	*	*	4
	1	0	1	2	
SUPOFF	*	*	*	*	4
	0	1	0	3	
NONE	22. 0%	2. 4%	4. 9%	70. 7%	41
	9	1	2	29	
TOTAL	16. 2%	9. 5%	8. 1%	66. 2%	74
	12	7	6	49	

Exclusion analysis:
Table total: 74
Excluded: 39
Sample size: 113

Table 206

How Enlisted Commanders (COMEN), Enlisted Supervisors
(SUPEN), Officer Commanders (COMOFF), Supervisory Of-
ficers (SUPOFF) and Those Holding No Position (NONE)
Perceived Leadership Elements Relative To Question # 146

"Tended to blame others for things he was supposed to do
when they went wrong "

RANTI BY BLAME

DOWN: Rank title
ACROSS: Blame others for errors

PERCENTAGES ACROSS

	OFF	NCO	WAR	ALL	TOTAL
COMEN	0. 0%	16. 7%	8. 3%	75. 0%	12
	0	2	1	9	
SUPEN	25. 0%	16. 7%	8. 3%	50. 0%	12
	3	2	1	6	
COMOFF	25. 0%	12. 5%	37. 5%	25. 0%	8
	2	1	3	2	
SUPOFF	*	*	*	*	3
	0	0	0	3	
NONE	12. 8%	15. 4%	10. 3%	61. 5%	39
	5	6	4	24	
TOTAL	13. 5%	14. 9%	12. 2%	59. 5%	74
	10	11	9	44	

Exclusion analysis:
Table total: 74
Excluded: 39
Sample size: 113

Table 207

How Enlisted Commanders (COMEN), Enlisted Supervisors
(SUPEN), Officer Commanders (COMOFF), Supervisory Of-
ficers (SUPOFF) and Those Holding No Position (NONE)
Perceived Leadership Elements Relative To Question # 147

"Stuck to the letter of his superiors orders"

RANTI BY STUCK

DOWN: Rank title
ACROSS: Stuck to letter orders

PERCENTAGES ACROSS

	OFF	NCO	WAR	ALL	TOTAL
COMEN	0. 0%	16. 7%	16. 7%	66. 7%	12
	0	2	2	8	
SUPEN	23. 1%	7. 7%	7. 7%	61. 5%	13
	3	1	1	8	
COMOFF	60. 0%	10. 0%	20. 0%	10. 0%	10
	6	1	2	1	
SUPOFF	*	*	*	*	4
	1	0	0	3	
NONE	15. 4%	5. 1%	2. 6%	76. 9%	39
	6	2	1	30	
TOTAL	20. 5%	7. 7%	7. 7%	64. 1%	78
	16	6	6	50	

Exclusion analysis:
Table total: 78
Excluded: 35
Sample size: 113

Table 208

How Enlisted Commanders (COMEN), Enlisted Supervisors (SUPEN), Officer Commanders (COMOFF), Supervisory Officers (SUPOFF), and Those Holding No Position (NONE) Perceived Leadership Elements Relative To Question # 151

RANTI BY SCALCO

"On a scale of from 1 to 10 in which 1 is the worst and 10 is the best, how well do you think your unit would do in actual combat"

DOWN: Rank title
ACROSS: Scale of combat ability

PERCENTAGES ACROSS

	1	2	3	4	5	6	7	8	9	10	TOTAL
COMEN	0.0% 0	0.0% 0	5.9% 1	5.9% 1	29.4% 5	17.6% 3	17.6% 3	11.8% 2	0.0% 0	11.8% 2	17
SUPEN	0.0% 0	0.0% 0	0.0% 0	25.0% 4	12.5% 2	18.7% 3	6.2% 1	31.2% 5	0.0% 0	6.2% 1	16
COMOFF	0.0% 0	0.0% 0	0.0% 0	33.3% 4	16.7% 2	0.0% 0	0.0% 0	33.3% 4	8.3% 1	8.3% 1	12
SUPOFF	0.0% 0	0.0% 0	12.5% 1	0.0% 0	25.0% 2	25.0% 2	37.5% 3	0.0% 0	0.0% 0	0.0% 0	8
NONE	5.7% 3	3.8% 2	30.2% 16	13.2% 7	11.3% 6	9.4% 5	17.0% 9	3.8% 2	1.9% 1	3.8% 2	53
TOTAL	2.8% 3	1.9% 2	17.0% 18	15.1% 16	16.0% 17	12.3% 13	15.1% 16	12.3% 13	1.9% 2	5.7% 6	106

Exclusion analysis:
Table total: 106
Excluded: 7
Sample size: 113

207

Table 209

How Enlisted Commanders (COMEN), Enlisted Supervisors
(SUPEN), Officer Commanders (COMOFF), Supervisory Of-
ficers (SUPOFF) and Those Holding No Position (NONE)
Perceived Leadership Elements Relative To Question # 156

"On a scale of from 1 to 10 in which 1 is the worst and
10 is the best, how would you rate the military training
your unit received"

RANTI BY TRAIN

DOWN: Rank title
ACROSS: Quality of training

PERCENTAGES ACROSS

	1	2	3	4	5	6	7	8	9	10	TOTAL
COMEN	0.0% 0	5.9% 1	11.8% 2	11.8% 2	23.5% 4	11.8% 2	11.8% 2	17.6% 3	0.0% 0	5.9% 1	17
SUPEN	0.0% 0	6.2% 1	0.0% 0	6.2% 1	12.5% 2	12.5% 2	18.7% 3	25.0% 4	12.5% 2	6.2% 1	16
COMOFF	0.0% 0	0.0% 0	0.0% 0	25.0% 3	8.3% 1	0.0% 0	33.3% 4	16.7% 2	0.0% 0	16.7% 2	12
SUPOFF	0.0% 0	0.0% 0	37.5% 3	12.5% 1	25.0% 2	0.0% 0	12.5% 1	12.5% 1	0.0% 0	0.0% 0	8
NONE	9.3% 5	11.1% 6	16.7% 9	3.7% 2	20.4% 11	5.6% 3	14.8% 8	11.1% 6	1.9% 1	5.6% 3	54
TOTAL	4.7% 5	7.5% 8	13.1% 14	8.4% 9	18.7% 20	6.5% 7	16.8% 18	15.0% 16	2.8% 3	6.5% 7	107

Exclusion analysis:
Table total: 107
Excluded: 6
Sample size: 113

208

Table 210

Type of Unit As A Background Variable for Question # 22

"About how much free time did you have to yourself in
an average week"

RANK BY FRETIM

DOWN: Highest rank
ACROSS: Free time

PERCENTAGES ACROSS

	HOURS	DAY	ALNONE	EVMIN	TIME	TOTAL
PRIV	32. 2%	22. 0%	15. 3%	8. 5%	22. 0%	59
	19	13	9	5	13	
NCO	37. 9%	27. 6%	17. 2%	6. 9%	10. 3%	29
	11	8	5	2	3	
WAR	*	*	*	*	*	3
	1	1	0	0	1	
OFF	25. 0%	20. 0%	30. 0%	0. 0%	25. 0%	20
	5	4	6	0	5	
TOTAL	32. 4%	23. 4%	18. 0%	6. 3%	19. 8%	111
	36	26	20	7	22	

Exclusion analysis:
Table total: 111
Excluded: 2
Sample size: 113

Table 211

Type of Unit As A Background Variable for Question # 51

"In the whole time you were in the military , how many
times were you allowed to leave the base for your own
recreation"

UNTYP BY OFPOST

DOWN: type of unit
ACROSS: # times allowed leave

PERCENTAGES ACROSS
============ ======

	1-2	3-5	6-10	+10	TOTAL
INFANT	20. 0%	8. 0%	8. 0%	64. 0%	25
	5	2	2	16	
TANKS	50. 0%	10. 0%	0. 0%	40. 0%	10
	5	1	0	4	
ARTLY	25. 0%	12. 5%	0. 0%	62. 5%	8
	2	1	0	5	
ROCKET	15. 0%	0. 0%	5. 0%	80. 0%	20
	3	0	1	16	
SUPUN	25. 0%	17. 9%	3. 6%	53. 6%	28
	7	5	1	15	
STAFF	*	*	*	*	4
	0	1	0	3	
OTHER	*	*	*	*	2
	0	0	0	2	
TOTAL	22. 7%	10. 3%	4. 1%	62. 9%	97
	22	10	4	61	

Exclusion analysis:
Table total: 97
Excluded: 16
Sample size: 113

Table 212

Type of Unit As A Background Variable for Question # 60

"Did anyone in your unit ever physically assault an officer"

UNTYP BY ASOFF

DOWN: type of unit
ACROSS: Assault an officer

PERCENTAGES ACROSS

	YES	NO	TOTAL
INFANT	39. 3%	60. 7%	28
	11	17	
TANKS	36. 4%	63. 6%	11
	4	7	
ARTLY	54. 5%	45. 5%	11
	6	5	
ROCKET	26. 1%	73. 9%	23
	6	17	
SUPUN	40. 0%	60. 0%	30
	12	18	
STAFF	*	*	4
	1	3	
OTHER	*	*	3
	1	2	
TOTAL	37. 3%	62. 7%	110
	41	69	

Exclusion analysis:
Table total: 110
Excluded: 3
Sample size: 113

Table 213

Type of Unit As A Background Variable for Question # 61

"Did anyone in your unit ever physically assault an
non-commissioned officer"

UNTYP BY ASNCO

DOWN: type of unit
ACROSS: Assault an NCO

PERCENTAGES ACROSS

	YES	NO	TOTAL
INFANT	48.3%	51.7%	29
	14	15	
TANKS	46.2%	53.8%	13
	6	7	
ARTLY	72.7%	27.3%	11
	8	3	
ROCKET	78.3%	21.7%	23
	18	5	
SUPUN	71.4%	28.6%	28
	20	8	
STAFF	*	*	4
	3	1	
OTHER	*	*	3
	2	1	
TOTAL	64.0%	36.0%	111
	71	40	

Exclusion analysis:
Table total: 111
Excluded: 2
Sample size: 113

Table 214

Type of Unit As A Background Variable for Question # 68

"Did you ever hear of or see an officer drunk on duty"

UNTYP BY DRUNK

DOWN: type of unit
ACROSS: Officer drunk

PERCENTAGES ACROSS

	YES	NO	TOTAL
INFANT	46.4%	53.6%	28
	13	15	
TANKS	41.7%	58.3%	12
	5	7	
ARTLY	63.6%	36.4%	11
	7	4	
ROCKET	69.6%	30.4%	23
	16	7	
SUPUN	65.5%	34.5%	29
	19	10	
STAFF	*	*	3
	1	2	
OTHER	*	*	3
	2	1	
TOTAL	57.8%	42.2%	109
	63	46	

Exclusion analysis:
Table total: 109
Excluded: 4
Sample size: 113

Table 215

Type of Unit As A Background Variable for Question # 69

"Did you ever hear of or see a non-commissioned officer
drunk on duty"

_____

UNTYP BY NCODNK

DOWN: type of unit
ACROSS: NCO drunk

PERCENTAGES ACROSS
============ ======

	YES	NO	TOTAL
INFANT	57.1%	42.9%	28
	16	12	
TANKS	66.7%	33.3%	12
	8	4	
ARTLY	81.8%	18.2%	11
	9	2	
ROCKET	81.8%	18.2%	22
	18	4	
SUPUN	66.7%	33.3%	27
	18	9	
STAFF	*	*	4
	2	2	
OTHER	*	*	3
	2	1	
TOTAL	68.2%	31.8%	107
	73	34	

Exclusion analysis:
Table total: 107
Excluded: 6
Sample size: 113

Table 216

Type of Unit As A Background Variable for Question # 84

"When you were in the military did anyone in your unit
ever commit suicide"

UNTYP BY KILL

DOWN: type of unit
ACROSS: Commit suicide

PERCENTAGES ACROSS

	YES	NO	TOTAL
INFANT	37.9%	62.1%	29
	11	18	
TANKS	50.0%	50.0%	12
	6	6	
ARTLY	36.4%	63.6%	11
	4	7	
ROCKET	65.2%	34.8%	23
	15	8	
SUPUN	51.7%	48.3%	29
	15	14	
STAFF	*	*	4
	2	2	
OTHER	*	*	3
	2	1	
TOTAL	49.5%	50.5%	111
	55	56	

Exclusion analysis:
Table total: 111
Excluded: 2
Sample size: 113

Table 217

Type of Unit As A Background Variable for Question # 85

"Did anyone in your unit ever attempt to commit suicide"

UNTYP BY ATKILL

DOWN: type of unit
ACROSS: Attempted suicide

PERCENTAGES ACROSS
============ ======

	YES	NO	TOTAL
INFANT	46.4%	53.6%	28
	13	15	
TANKS	58.3%	41.7%	12
	7	5	
ARTLY	54.5%	45.5%	11
	6	5	
ROCKET	68.2%	31.8%	22
	15	7	
SUPUN	53.6%	46.4%	28
	15	13	
STAFF	*	*	3
	2	1	
OTHER	*	*	3
	2	1	
TOTAL	56.1%	43.9%	107
	60	47	

Exclusion analysis:
Table total: 107
Excluded: 6
Sample size: 113

Table 218

Type of Unit As A Background Variable for Question # 98

"Given the general quality of officers that you served
with in your military service, how would you rate their
quality as officers"

UNTYP BY OFQUAL

DOWN: type of unit
ACROSS: Officer quality

PERCENTAGES ACROSS
======================

	EXGOOD	GOOD	AVG	FAIR	POOR	VPOOR	TOTAL
INFANT	3.6%	3.6%	67.9%	7.1%	14.3%	3.6%	28
	1	1	19	2	4	1	
TANKS	0.0%	15.4%	46.2%	23.1%	15.4%	0.0%	13
	0	2	6	3	2	0	
ARTLY	0.0%	9.1%	72.7%	9.1%	9.1%	0.0%	11
	0	1	8	1	1	0	
ROCKET	0.0%	21.7%	39.1%	26.1%	8.7%	4.3%	23
	0	5	9	6	2	1	
SUPUN	0.0%	3.4%	55.2%	13.8%	27.6%	0.0%	29
	0	1	16	4	8	0	
STAFF	*	*	*	*	*	*	4
	0	0	4	0	0	0	
OTHER	*	*	*	*	*	*	3
	0	1	2	0	0	0	
TOTAL	0.9%	9.9%	57.7%	14.4%	15.3%	1.8%	111
	1	11	64	16	17	2	

Exclusion analysis:
Table total: 111
Excluded: 2
Sample size: 113

Table 219

Type of Unit As A Background Variable for Question # 99

"How would you rate the quality of the non-commissioned
officers you came into contact with"

UNTYP BY NCOQUAL

DOWN: type of unit
ACROSS: NCO quality

PERCENTAGES ACROSS

	EXGOOD	GOOD	AVG	FAIR	POOR	VPOOR	TOTAL
INFANT	7.1%	21.4%	50.0%	10.7%	7.1%	3.6%	
	2	6	14	3	2	1	
TANKS	0.0%	23.1%	46.2%	23.1%	7.7%	0.0%	
	0	3	6	3	1	0	
ARTLY	0.0%	9.1%	63.6%	18.2%	0.0%	9.1%	
	0	1	7	2	0	1	
ROCKET	0.0%	30.4%	26.1%	26.1%	13.0%	4.3%	
	0	7	6	6	3	1	
SUPUN	0.0%	6.9%	48.3%	24.1%	13.8%	6.9%	
	0	2	14	7	4	2	
STAFF	*	*	*	*	*	*	
	0	0	2	2	0	0	
OTHER	*	*	*	*	*	*	
	0	2	1	0	0	0	
TOTAL	1.8%	18.9%	45.0%	20.7%	9.0%	4.5%	1
	2	21	50	23	10	5	

Exclusion analysis:
Table total: 111
Excluded: 2
Sample size: 113

Table 220

Type of Unit As A Background Variable for Question # 102

"When you were in the military did anyone in your unit
ever desert"

UNTYP BY DSRT

DOWN: type of unit
ACROSS: Desertion

PERCENTAGES ACROSS
============ ======

	YES	NO	TOTAL
INFANT	55.6%	44.4%	27
	15	12	
TANKS	76.9%	23.1%	13
	10	3	
ARTLY	45.5%	54.5%	11
	5	6	
ROCKET	22.7%	77.3%	22
	5	17	
SUPUN	58.6%	41.4%	29
	17	12	
STAFF	*	*	4
	3	1	
OTHER	*	*	3
	1	2	
TOTAL	51.4%	48.6%	109
	56	53	

Exclusion analysis:
Table total: 109
Excluded: 4
Sample size: 113

Table 221

Type of Unit As A Background Variable for Question # 103

"Did you ever hear of an officer deserting"

UNTYP BY OFFDRT

DOWN: type of unit
ACROSS: Officer desertion

PERCENTAGES ACROSS
=========== ======

	YES	NO	TOTAL
INFANT	22. 2%	77. 8%	27
	6	21	
TANKS	15. 4%	84. 6%	13
	2	11	
ARTLY	30. 0%	70. 0%	10
	3	7	
ROCKET	4. 3%	95. 7%	23
	1	22	
SUPUN	17. 2%	82. 8%	29
	5	24	
STAFF	*	*	4
	0	4	
OTHER	*	*	3
	0	3	
TOTAL	15. 6%	84. 4%	109
	17	92	

Exclusion analysis:
Table total: 109
Excluded: 4
Sample size: 113

Table 222

Type of Unit As A Background Variable for Question # 105

"Did you ever hear of a non-commissioned officer deserting"

UNTYP BY NCODRT

DOWN: type of unit
ACROSS: NCO desertion

PERCENTAGES ACROSS
========== ======

	YES	NO	TOTAL
INFANT	60. 7%	39. 3%	28
	17	11	
TANKS	61. 5%	38. 5%	13
	8	5	
ARTLY	50. 0%	50. 0%	10
	5	5	
ROCKET	65. 2%	34. 8%	23
	15	8	
SUPUN	75. 9%	24. 1%	29
	22	7	
STAFF	*	*	4
	3	1	
OTHER	*	*	3
	2	1	
TOTAL	65. 5%	34. 5%	110
	72	38	

Exclusion analysis:
Table total: 110
Excluded: 3
Sample size: 113

Table 223

Type of Unit As A Background Variable for Question # 111

"In general, is going absent without leave a big problem
in the military"

UNTYP BY PROBA

DOWN: type of unit
ACROSS: AWOL a big problem

PERCENTAGES ACROSS
=========== ======

	YES	NO	TOTAL
INFANT	85.7%	14.3%	28
	24	4	
TANKS	84.6%	15.4%	13
	11	2	
ARTLY	70.0%	30.0%	10
	7	3	
ROCKET	80.0%	20.0%	20
	16	4	
SUPUN	86.2%	13.8%	29
	25	4	
STAFF	*	*	4
	3	1	
OTHER	*	*	3
	1	2	
TOTAL	81.3%	18.7%	107
	87	20	

Exclusion analysis:
Table total: 107
Excluded: 6
Sample size: 113

222

Table 224

Type of Unit As A Background Variable for Question # 112

"Is desertion a big problem in the military"

UNTYP BY PROBD

DOWN: type of unit
ACROSS: Desertion a big problem

PERCENTAGES ACROSS
============ ======

	YES	NO	TOTAL
INFANT	57.1%	42.9%	28
	16	12	
TANKS	38.5%	61.5%	13
	5	8	
ARTLY	80.0%	20.0%	10
	8	2	
ROCKET	30.0%	70.0%	20
	6	14	
SUPUN	51.9%	48.1%	27
	14	13	
STAFF	*	*	4
	3	1	
OTHER	*	*	3
	2	1	
TOTAL	51.4%	48.6%	105
	54	51	

Exclusion analysis:
Table total: 105
Excluded: 8
Sample size: 113

223

Table 225

Type of Unit As A Background Variable for Question # 156

"On a scale of from 1 to 10 in which 1 is the worst and
10 is the best, how would you rate the military training
your unit received"

UNTYP BY TRAIN

DOWN: type of unit
ACROSS: Quality of training

PERCENTAGES ACROSS

	1	2	3	4	5	6	7	8	9	10	TOTAL
INFANT	3.6% 1	7.1% 2	14.3% 4	10.7% 3	10.7% 3	7.1% 2	28.6% 8	10.7% 3	0.0% 0	7.1% 2	28
TANKS	0.0% 0	0.0% 0	23.1% 3	7.7% 1	23.1% 3	0.0% 0	7.7% 1	23.1% 3	0.0% 0	15.4% 2	13
ARTLY	0.0% 0	0.0% 0	0.0% 0	27.3% 3	9.1% 1	18.2% 2	9.1% 1	18.2% 2	0.0% 0	18.2% 2	11
ROCKET	0.0% 0	9.1% 2	4.5% 1	4.5% 1	22.7% 5	13.6% 3	13.6% 3	13.6% 2	13.6% 3	4.5% 1	22
SUPUN	14.8% 4	14.8% 4	22.2% 6	3.7% 1	22.2% 6	0.0% 0	11.1% 3	11.1% 3	0.0% 0	0.0% 0	27
STAFF	* 1	* 0	* 0	* 0	* 0	* 0	* 1	* 2	* 0	* 0	4
OTHER	* 0	* 0	* 0	* 0	* 2	* 0	* 1	* 0	* 0	* 0	3
TOTAL	5.6% 6	7.4% 8	13.0% 14	8.3% 9	18.5% 20	6.5% 7	16.7% 18	14.8% 16	2.8% 3	6.5% 7	108

Exclusion analysis:
Table total: 108
Excluded: 5
Sample size: 113

Table 226

Ordinal Categories Of Perceptions Of Combat Ability Of Soviet Units

	N	%
High (8-10)	21	18.6
Medium (4-7)	63	56.6%
Low (1-3)	23	20.4%

Table 227

Ordinal Categories Of Perceptions Of The Quality Of Soviet Training

	N	%
High (8-10)	26	23.1
Medium (4-7)	54	47.8
Low (1-3)	28	23.1

Raw
Data
Files _____

```
118102687053531112112827215311221212222132112251111218202012212252111132121212121
118221512123211322462113111211888434462222531231312115455454545441545554
1183531542950030724203204

027101717253632263215827215311225112222132221224122221800202222132121231122112223121
02722241112221121242221422121253535562221111123111111552544151541451144414454444
0273455444990130504201202

026102697153632263445821215311225212131122331121123311121112113390000212335253612111122222111
026211312121211242214122253333339993346222253129231122135311155515551115555555555155
02635555550000030608201303

022102687054632113433813215311222121313211141121240200212213242611121111113121
02221141111121142111999445412214251112141144455354445354445545545
02234544459010204061062 04

019102727775342121313171311532125122221132125244112228010022222252415251131111221111
01921132211121131114511412221199992234222225112522251111151515552525244545555545
0193525445503010803202207

017103656854321113151812215311131212122152111121111190070212221221221411211111321
0172222111112112214221142212129999444122225112312125511511512155515253535345151115355515
0173555111900510412210207
```

013211112213131312124211321111299995635112241129222115535555521523255521332555525
0133555534000020322201201

0101027274546322134458132153332212122232132111131112280150222112141511112311113221
0102114121221111311125331222133399977673331221111333131111111123241555523
01034222549505107081032048

0071026871545321134358122153121221212222113221222512122806002222251415352132222131 21
0072114222221212214522132222212999944422222144125121224514444435114454445115544553 1
00734135319505208062012078

0061027117353442213255127225312112212222322222225222222806002112252112131112121226122
006211312122311311314221219999933361222144123111141113531143542412551455545 5
0063544554801010605201208

0011027117251532213253281221531222121222262121211111180032211121212112251141322142 11
00121311112112224522141212339999555612225312311121544515555255545444545455541
001355544590103030820210 3

0551026870536322534448112153122522222252211313121212228015021222324151631412121212 1
05521141211111122352114221211999924562221431231212154445451115555455544431554 1
0553515444855307102032058

229

043102747653422153154811215311151212222422211121218020022212114151212121111121
043211312111111114111121111111999922332111222125111121111341111131131155131
043332343199053101221021010

035102676953321253214827215311122121212222522223311111802802212231415153111113221
035211311111111222451112222232999953551221411231113115441455554515444143531
035341142440301041520210610

052101737374545322132138132253221132122222522211212113800000211121111111313212
052211222111211211311124322139999333422242127111115154354155515342511553110
052315443300001051020220205

050101697054321263155812215311112121212131322211118020022112221112111151110
050211311211112121151113222199995645122241123111225555555555555555555555510
050335555500003000030030010

049102687053322213155812215312141421222421111211211180100122122221122522231222132121
049211412111132141121222221199993256222253127111115111543321251135521131111155521
049352243499023051020320710

044102727453332111315581322553121413122262221131211180120211224251111123222
044222511111111211411113121212999993354122143137111215514422453554121114351441541
044332342499011030210310310

0311243964532122132128272152121312222162121243311280000112221242526313312211121
0312225123231112112411124112223331999924561221111371111113411555333123111131251513344551
0353343440005310141105210

0281105565533211134328111234328212232122311322124411221801202022215251412113121212121
0282115111123213114322142112221999923311214313231112311121115514444151111515115151
0283211522950510806203208

0951027070725332116315581421511225121211213211213111218020022212514212311212121214221
0952213111111112142221422121199993354221431251111554153315151513551355335511
0953155115000023040420111102

0941026565753321213444282721531213121202222522221212121118000021122425162521312222143333
0942336333336336335363333363333362999933462222251372211155115555515555555555555555
0943555555000003030620012032

0911036265534211631558163153122511222222232211331111180100022221223161111311133121
0912112221123113214511132111119999335122122123112121115514445555154314544444441445
0913455555990110204101012032

0881036466753321153154827215314822212122213212141212380500022222524151515121224221
0882113211112122245111422221199993336222154123112215544335354341435544443445541
0883225224950510300201205

087103666953321263215812213312241212224121122111229000022222232415141111216221
08721121112211111145221422212219999332412214311271111312521135155312133311154425
08735552239802306022201203

086102687054322132164131133121312122223212123121218020011122122132521111113111
086211111121111214211141212119999332612214112711111524454525155414555444445544
086355544598021051142011 08

085102737553531213151814215312221222216222121211111801602212232121252141222132 21
08521243221132122135111421123339999333612213512322155135155555451535555544
085355541470301030220 3103

077102727373532253154827215312251222221321123511222803002222252415133231222221 23
077222533122211511362214122233999625622225592512155555555555555555555555555555
0773555558004307242 0 2207

075101757654312134318272153121221112121213211321111901202111132536121233321222 121
0752225221121121212322414122229999325612214312311121221131242122141222112121 1211
0753255555000040804106107

074101717253632253154827215312121232122262221222211380150222222212226311121234 111
074211212113111222442221532333299993656122141199331115544545554135455553413455 52
07435553459802301052013 02

0731026867543222531548272153122112211521115111112800002222252314151112122112121
0732113131131212511142212229999235422214312321122154424454312551145524441255541
0733332442802030606108207

0701026666853421243154827215312152121222262222114121118001222222524151412311114221
0702114142111111121421111211112129999355612212212522121554455455545545454445445554
0703555444901010410201208

0671036567536321631558122153123521223321622114221118015022211514152521212221421
0672113211233113214121142212129999534612212212332221155115553145551534435445544
0673555444000003031220110 3

0691027374546322131518122153121512122226222321312113800075222224121314112122132 21
0692225211111221452313212229999335622213112721151345153551125325521
0693552424000030310201203

0661027171735374221344581222531112121221144222133111111801002322231516152232111122221
0662134222111162142221512122229994446222153127111225555555555555555555555555555555
0663555555000004070420130 5

0601026971544222631558142153121511122223122121211803002121122416131111111114211
0602112111111122451121112119999335612212112321112544453515515455535155555555555555
0603555555901030304202101

233

11910366653742243224812153122212122262222113121118010021112141512111111111121
11922141211131311411141142111229999323622214112312321111111111111132313331551
1193111333900510812201208

11510364675352126315581521531221121222252222112121118060021132314151311211114211
11521121212211222411111211111229999551111111119922112153334343351554534445541
11535551459802102042013o1

0561036164533211631568271153122511222216221215221180120212215241511123221125221
0562325121111122145211332212229999345612221341231112145341351555335325533355545
05634531359901304062013o1

12810271725353221315181121531112121222221522211211122802002122224231336313122214221
12821131113311121143221422121299995556222253123121215534542551555545554133445542
12835554440000303032012o2

12210366685321114311482721532115121221132111322122800002112232415132131212232121
12221131111211222421113221211999933351221123111112244454541154454534444444544
1223454445901030510101105

12110263664533211131577162143121212121222115211224111380100222222524152524322223123
12122252312353331145221622131399993346222111199212115545353515555511555511
1213555111990110420201205

234

11310363665421128311541321531212121212122242111121112280000222123241514111212121213111
11321121212112112224111622121119995455122144125111115444545454554431445544
11335554448010106102023305

10210460604534212133328122153122211222221321112222118001222222121212522513111 2221
10222252211111211145112121221999933621222639971111551353535355155521355335551
10235555530001104252011205

10110270725342115311481212531125122222152111111112280100222222424151513111112211
10121131112211132111311111119999443522212712121111254515255554415544224435535
10131112529901107052081 03

10010266685332115312481311123111112121311321112213221180022522212222415131121121 123221
10021131212221132135111313122212999944352221421231215411232112514545552234145 441
10033252549505104052022 04

09910267695332113152816215312142212231211111111800045211111511111111222112 11
09921131211111211442214122129999425612214112311211444545455555554444455554
09935554440008110142011 10

00210542472411221322538122153131313121222262222111111180000021112112125215111112111
00221112111111211245111121111199995355131411127111115555555555555555555555555
00235555500003080001 08210

```
004107435023111153154811225312111222222622211131211180015211112514122111113121
004211322212221221151114211219999545612221441271111111111511555511551155115541
00434551410000303062011 02


003107435021211132528132153121112222242221111111180060212221222521312221 2121
003221421111111114511242122119999433122244312711111155444451455114551125 1513511 55541
003355152499011070410320 8


018105404523321213433812225321131122311321122512222280110222225241513124122 322213
018222513311633611342225333333399992255123255235212551222441155455555525255555511
0183511511950530910110110


025104404424211273211816225312121212122311322134222138006022222524141512 1222 23111
025222511111112121214122219997933242225439921111555555555555555555555555555555
025355555500004000003003 00


030102484924211163155827215312231212222622211211211802002112221221325212 1111 14121
030222522112111214511142111119999546111442123111211544542551554555444454 4445 44
0303555444802030324202102


032106404623321213211827337433361212212522133633333900003333393900003333633 3333
032233633336332111123122113399997767333367933333333141424455225415555555 5226333
0333425555955051050020130 8
```

236

054106434924421113152813221312131232125212211213121113121111
05421131212332332144221422222999934412214223722222555555545455455541
0543555544950530612201205

0461044245232122131518161273121112122224221111121280200211221242212422251222213121
04622152121212135221433232999324122223127111111114111112111111111111
046311211100003030010510 5

0581044146231112134318161212125223111612122121111802002322524151113322311131
05822251112142141451213321999911111123113127112125555111155151555555555555
0583555551901041000201110

0611054248231122131518132253121112222222322111322121800002222231214222221212 1
061222512222242242145222533333339999934342222255127111135555555555555555555 5
0613555555000030406203205

0341045054233212331575272253121112122226222115111118005021222515151312121112 1
0342121211313111411151212119999324122411232111553544155135445415555444455555
0343455444901010002203205

0421044246231122132218132273211221221113122223221218002511121324151212512222 1
042221511121511411161115322221999932322222568111115512122122511222141114224222 2
0423444440000110061102 10

```
09810240404223111221341181321531212122122222232221131221280000222222222416131131213131 4221
0982214111112121122145221411232299995325111122236211115444454555555444445555
0983555554901010310201104


10410540452332226315582721531224121222142111152211180045322225222132421412122221 21
1042225222121112242122141124242122219999236122141123111215544515254244445525354445454544
10435254444000011062020202205


07110247492342126315581121531211212121222622221132111280300022222225241513112122222 4122
0712225222121132232142142122299993345122243123121115544554524554424455545
0713554449505030310201201


08310640462363121343381621531113321222226222211111118012021222211213141151111 13222
0832114211124112421312111212222299993351112336711221524411252124414242414144444444
0833222444200520040810320 4


09110441452342121343381322122113212211116233222322380000332225362522532222212 11
09122251212363363452225333339999363322356999933331145111111111155554555551
0913111551000040500201204


09710343462332121344182725312121222221522112221111800021222224151511121111 13211
0972112111123123214221142111219999356111122127111111155445155444555441542551 4
0973555444199013052420011 07
```

112105414623421263445814226622213312222151211332222228000023221521211411632222222222
112222412122531521511225333111999954331122564999331115555555555555555555555555555
1123555555000040000300

116102434521212133225212215332113212222522221122211380010213224241516116323336221
1162336333116336223423163333339999333421316499993333155555555555555555555555555
116355555500004040030 2102

123105464502421121332281121211111212122262121121211180400021222224151311123111112121
123222512111111214111131211219999535511214443991112155445425544455441454545 44
1233255444950530703201205

125105414523631213211816122122222211222222522113222121800182222252421131122222212122
125222312111311311142216333333999952231212545711112114212411142541155551555555
125312155585071100720920208

124103505323111263561813225318132225312121222222216222113111118030022222521214112111123221
124211312112322322452212213339999665633314212313121554454554545554445115544
124352241495051041210320 1

008100358614353121321281221531225122121222142221131211802000222224251512111121213211
0082113121112214511212221299993356112141123121215544545454545544445445544
0883555445000010500201205

239

```
014103660634442227321181322531212121212222422211311113800002222222415141113111122 2111
0142114121222113131214121211999932232121421271111111524545551511153454554455545
01434244549505108162042 0 7

020102662634421124315481222153111111221212522121111211803002112232121252111212242 1 21
020211112111112214122112212121199993556222251112911111155413555545455153444 1115 15
0203455444490101071220120 5

0231036616443421263155827215312151112221622211211111807003112152415131111111611 1
0232112111111112111411112222221999933112222141271213155445155555445555455554 45545
02335555559770310004210200

0451036606342421213151815215312211212122155221111111180060212221241514111212241 11
0452113121111121451113221221999933131214114112311111115441545245544455444544554 5 545
0453555444490103011010410 4203

062102575943321213223812122111112222311312122412123800080222225141514225121 11331 1
0622115121121132135212532222199993334222254135112115542423515351455544541 5 5542
06235532248020106122022 06

0801025960043421213151827215312223121222242112121211212800048222222525212621332221212 1
080222422311211321242215111222999943452222551271112123115122511515552221 2255 11
080325244390101050810720 6
```

0791035861434212531248272153122112112211142212232212180450222225241513131312222121
07921132212121321442214222119999342214213231121554134255555555555555551
07932224459010308072002209

0821025596044321163155813221312122212222242221122211122422412111212121
08222241111321311312214211112199994324222142223711114444144444445444435 44
082345444490101051220520 5

0841025757584332226322382721532221122231132111252221180100222222141515124121212121
084221412111111232214112119999342422224412811111112511521412111222212 51155
0843111252950820807102208

1061035963434212531548272132121212122242111131231380000233223353623341222221 11
10621143311211252135131321333399999434432222621293333112255555555555555555 55
106355555500004000003003 00

120103576043322143155813215131315322211422212222122218025012222121212125225122212122
12021251211211211352115221222299993322122214512311111111145451141151514511344155555 1
120351144490101050805205

1091133447132122134468162133121112222214211112112212180182122242424142412222221
10922251212231321421212219999335622224512311111511144555454545544454455 44
1093555444990110612201208

241

```
0221035366333212134318112151311112121222132212121212122228100022222231411121112211221221
0222214121112121214522253333331999932551221411291212151111131511111141121212225 21
0223551111990110804201208

0121035053334211112258162253121112121222152111212111800002212254151211212121 21
0122113221121421445121422122229999542612214112332112222115524515522245222115511
0123533111900310510201108

1141013536134222132268272213122312122231211213132221800080212222222415121312122221
1142214212211221452311231212999934561211111135222212555122222552455525224255 51
11435524249505104202021 07

0651023335131122131518271122222211222113221225111118000801222231421262131222222122
0652113121223232145111222212999933241111128121111225211251255515522512215 42
06531154540000305102022 04

0401033538133312132138122212222141212022252222111211118000502112211526252121221231 11
0402212111224112114222222221199993322222224127111125544255545544545544445 5444
0403444444000830618203206

0111023436121122131518271213221112132211121212222528002421122125132313122223211
0112224121112111145225332212999931242222211232111555444545555544455544444 544
0113555445900530520201202
```

0211035555833422213151812222311211212122213222114111228100011122524151411131112222111
02121141313123311312353111999793434222253125121212545242221141124225121545555
0213222152950130706203106

0331035255533112253154812221531212121222224222112221128003022222224151411412122311
033222242122221122145111321113211321199993245223243121554455452214554552212545554
03335154219801307102020108

0371025454563342221315181321531213131212222422211111111801802122124151313111112231 21
03722252211111121142111322121299993356222141123121115145245455551155511111111514
037355544010230310201203

0391035457333222132258272153122121212222321111322122800070212222223252111222121 21
03921131211211311412225333333399992434222421271111155115115425554455515
03935225549505108122203207

0471035457341115315482733742322132223113222313331222380020133325353613124121226332
047223633332133145222633333339999454622215529913311511522155211555555555525
0473555559010101110201307

0591035535633212131315381321531211212122223112121111118008021112515262621111212121 21
0592112121111112125221422123339999344421214112711115544554415544541442145552 1
05935554445000003079010530 7

0811263258333222134318162153121511122213131223361121180300213224222416114131323121
0812114121113134234511142113139999333213145399111111455444144155114441555545545
0813415551000040421101207

0721045054341122131548122253121112122222111121312222800401112232415251211222222122
0722225111112111211111142212229999221622225112511111212554524452552522221225525
0723222124900510724207206

0761025565834421113152827224311131222222252113341211280180212225212222521532222223223
0762224213123213234222153212329999445412214637222215544554555544554455445545544
0763555454920610406201103

0921035655931321213153827215312121212222422111211111180120212222214151411221131312222
0922113121112112133511122231199993551131221123111115152121225222522112522221524
0923144444990120904204208

0931025557333212131518132153131213131212221321111412222800702122252415141131222123121
0932115221111122145221112121219999334612214123111215521555244551551515555555555
0933522555980230712201307

0961065157345322634445816133112521221161212252111180120212211241513134221223221
0962215223122112214111153333219999444352221451231112222551454554555545455455545
0963555555500001050602303

110103555833421113255811215312223122222214211312111180150233325241513112123312221
110213322111211122224521142133329999354512334212312121551151515154541545445554
11034545454000040707201108

111104505333531112151816125321231122232132212111111180150222223131314112111113121
111211412111211221211111221121199995252121121127311132541242454545455555555555555
11135555559901103061071004

117102565657337421312282722253121412122213221151221180100222222524151412412221211
117221511112312311451114221121999934622224329911111112414554151412145222122211133
117344431190101081020012088

126103535733531243214812221531121122221142213321211180300021222114151311211112211
126221512112111114511112222229999335622252123322112244515551554554445444445541
12635554444950530706201205

105103553563333212532244827115311252222122262122222111218015021122224151512111332221
105222422111222121125111332221299994435222231123222215544544542454545544445445544
10534545449010206141071066

107103555583333222131518122153121111212221322121221221800301222222524151212122121121
107222512121211311422113221219999222512212212611112121551522225111515155455454555
10731425549005106102032077

```
1301026769524211532248161253112112222212322122311801502122222141513212122213121
1302114121212412414222141111199924342222232123111121134354144311542131532453454 2
13031445448010104102201209

1311035356363121333181221531211121222166221131211180300211122141524212111113211
13121111211112214222142212129999333422225212322225511313551111311131112533
13133333339010105122201207

1321035760436312131558152153122211222232322111411211805002222524161312312232211
132222512112321421351113221212999933352214312522111454444445455554455444545455555
1323555454801010304203205

1331027273534222531548142133122112122222622111112222280300222221252626216121111221
13321142221132132143125522221199994234222145127111225535232553543545424333335544
133355234495051080220110 9

1341027072536321132228161153112212122232321133122111805002221241116142221111222121
13421131212112141111412321199992214122124112311121251124432544535535243553553 2255
13434431118805106151104207
```

Bibliography _____

Books

Armstrong, John A. *Ideology, Politics and Government in the Soviet Union.* rev. ed. New York: Praeger, 1967

Babenko, I. *Soviet Officers (Sovetskiye Komandiry).* Moscow: Progress Publishers, 1976.

Baranov, V.I., ed. *Textbook on Educating Young Soldiers (Posobiye po pbucheniyu mododykh soldat).* Moscow: Voyenizdat, 1972.

Borzenko, Sergey O. *Soldiers of the 1970s (Soldaty semidesyatykh godov).* Moscow: Sovetskaya Rossiya, 1973.

Conner, Walter D. *Deviance in Soviet Society.* New York: Columbia University press, 1972.

Danchenko, A.M., and I.F. Vydrin, eds. *Military Pedagogy: A Soviet View (Voyennaya pedagogika).* Moscow: Voyenizdat, 1973.

Dictionary of Basic Military Terms: A Soviet View. Moscow: Voyenizdat, 1964.

Disciplinary Regulations of the U.S.S.R. Armed Forces (Distiplinarnyy ustav vooruzhennykh sil soyuza SSR). Moscow: Voyenizdat, 1971.

Dyachenko, Yevgeniy. *The Soviet Army.* Moscow: Novosti Press Agency Publishing House, 1974.

Erickson, John. *Soviet Military Performance: Some Manpower and Managerial Constraints.* New York: U.S. Army Institute for Advanced Russian Studies, 1970.

_____. *Soviet Armed Forces: Capabilities and Changing Roles.* Edinburgh: Defense Studies, Studies, University of Edinburgh, 1971.

_____. *Soviet Military Power.* London: Royal United Services Institute for Defense Studies, 1971.

_____. *The Soviet Military, Soviet Policy, and Soviet Politics.* Washington, D.C.: U.S. Strategic Institute, 1973.

Fialatov, V.I., ed. *Profession—Political Worker. Collection of Articles (Professiya—polirabornik. Sbornik staty).* Moscow: Voyenizdat, 1973.

General Military Regulations of the U.S.S.R. Armed Forces. (Obshchevoinskiye ustavy vooruzhennykh sil SSSR) Moscow: Voyenizdat, 1972.

Gittleman, Zvi. *Assimilation, Acculturation, and National Consciousness Among Soviet Jews.* Mimeographed. Ann Arbor, Mich.: University of Michigan, December 1972.

Goldhammer, Herbert. *The Soviet Soldier: Soviet Military Management at the Troop Level.* New York: Crane, Russak, 1975.

Gulidov, Afansiy I. *In the Combat Tradition (Na boyevykh tradisykh)*. Moscow: DOSAAF Press, 1974.

Goure, Leon. *The Military Indoctrination of Soviet Youth*. New York: National Strategy Information Center, 1973.

Grechko, Andrey Antonovich. *Armed Forces of the Soviet States (Vooruzhennyye sily sovetsko-go gosudarstva)*. Moscow: Voyenizdat, 1974.

Katz, Zev, Rosemarie Rogers, and Fredric Harned. *Handbook of Major Soviet Nationalities*. New York: Free Press, 1975.

Keefe, Eugene K. et al. *Area Handbook for Soviet Union*. Washington, D.C.: U.S. Government Printing Office, 1971.

Khmel, A. Ye., General Lieutenant. *Education of a Soviet Soldier: Party-Political Work in the Soviet Armed Forces*. Moscow:.Progress Publishers, 1972.

Kitov, Akhmed Ismaylovich, ed. *The Modern Army and Discipline (Sovremennaya armiya i distsiplina)*. Moscow: Voyenizdat, 1976.

Kochan, Lionel, ed. *The Jews of Soviet Russia 1917*. London: Oxford University Press, 1970.

Kolkowicz, Roman. *The Soviet Military and the Communist Party*. Princeton, N.J.: Princeton University Press, 1967.

Korey, William. *The Soviet Cage: Anti-Semitism in Russia*. New York: Viking Press, 1973.

Kovalev, Vladimir Nifolayvich. *Discipline is a Factor of Victory (Distiplina-faktor pobedy)*. Moscow: Voyenizdat, 1974.

Lototskiy, V.K. *The Soviet Army*. Moscow: Progress Publishers, 1971.

Marxism-Leninism on War and the Army. Moscow: Progress Publishers, 1972.

Myagkov, Aleksei. *Inside the KGB: An Exposé by an Officer of the Third Directorate*. London: The Foreign Affairs Publishing Company, 1977.

O'Ballance, Edgar. *The Red Army*. New York: Praeger, 1964.

Odom, William E. *The Soviet Volunteers*. Princeton, N.J.: Princeton University Press, 1973.

The Philosophical Heritage of V. I. Lenin and Problems of Contemporary War. Moscow: Military Publishing House, Voyenizdat, 1972.

Raygorodetsky, Yepim Yakovich. *Soldiers of the Seventies (Soldaty semidesyatykh)*. Moscow: DOSAAF Press, 1975.

Record, Jeffery. *Sizing Up the Soviet Army*. Washington, D.C.: The Brookings Institution, 1975.

Rendulic, Lothar. *Command and Control of the Troops (Upravleniye voyskami)*. Moscow: Government Printing House, 1972.

Savskin, V. Ye. *The Basic Principles of Operational Art and Tactics: A Soviet View*. Moscow: Ministry of Defense, 1972.

Seaton, Albert. *The Soviet Army*. Reading, Penn.: Osprey Publishing, Inc., 1972.

Shlyag, Y.V., A.D. Goltchkin, and K.K. Platonov. *Military Psychology: A Soviet View*. Moscow: Voyenizdat, 1973.

Shramchenko, A.F. *Psychology Problems in Command and Control of the Troops (Voprosy psikhologii v upravlenii voyskami)*. Moscow: Voyenizdat, 1973.

Sidoreko, A.A. *The Offensive: A Soviet View*. Washington, D.C.: Trans. Dept. of the Air Force, 1970.

Soviet Dynamics: Political, Economic Military. Pittsburgh: World Affairs Council, 1978.

Staritsyn, V.S., ed. *The Soviet Officer (A Collection of Articles. Introductory Article by Minister of Defense of the U.S.S.R., Marshal Andrey Grechko)*. Moscoe: Voyenizdat, 1970.

Structure of Discipline in the Soviet Army. Garmsch-Partenkirchken, West Germany: Army Institute for Advanced Russian Studies, 1975.

The U.S.S.R. In Figures for 1976. Moscow: Statisika Publishers, 1977.

Volkogonov, D.A. *Military Ethics (Voinskaya etika)*. Moscow: Voyenizdat, 1976.

Yerzunov, M.M., ed. *Warrant Officers and Naval Warrant Officers. A Collection of Articles (Praporstichiki i michmani. Sbornik statey)*. Moscow: Voyenizdat, 1973.

Articles

Altshuter, Mordekhai. "Mixed Marriages Amongst Soviet Jews." *Soviet Jewish Affairs*, De cember 1970.

Averin, A. "Improve Procedure." *Voyennyye Znaniya [Military Thought]*, February 1978.

Bedzhanyan, A., Major. "Indifference." *Krasnaya Zvezda [Red Star]*, 4 August 1977.

Belonozhko, S. "Commander of a Regiment." *Krasnava Zvezda [Red Star]*, 31 July 1976.

Bogdanovski, V. "In the Interests of the Service?" *Krasnava Zvezda [Red Star]*, 21 July 1976.

Boleylev, S. "For the Further Raising of the Quality and Effectiveness of Party Political Work." *Vestnik PVO [PVO Herald]*, 1976.

Boroukov, A. "Promotion." *Krasnaya Zvezda [Red Star]*, 8 April 1977.

Borisov, K. "Whom Is It Necessary to Defend?" *Krasnaya Zvezda [Red Star]*, 30 November 1976.

Choron, Jacques. "Concerning Suicide in Soviet Russia." *Bulletin of Suicidology*, December 1968.

Colton T.J. "Civil-Military Relations in Soviet Politics." *Current History*, October 1974.

Colshko, I. "Profoundly Know and Exactly Fulfill the Requirements of the New Troop Regula- tions." *Tyli Snabzhenie Sovietskikh Vooryzhennykh Sil [Soviet Supply Defense]*, 11 November 1975.

Druzhinin, M. "Responsibility of an Officer." *Voennii Vestnik [Military Herald]*, September 1977.

Glotov, V., and Oleinik, A. "Requirements of Discipline—A Law." *Voennii Vestnik [Military Herald]*, 3 (1977).

Golovnev, L. "An Outbreak of Anger." *Krasnaya Zvezda [Red Star]*, 9 October 1976.

Goncharov, V. "Position and Authority." *Krasnaya Zvezda [Red Star]*, 28 August 1976.

Gorny, A. "Socialist Legality and Soldierly Discipline." *Krasnaya Zvezda [Red Star]*, 1 Novem- ber 1974.

———. "Observing the Requirements of Laws and Regulations. "*Krasnaya Zvezda [Red Star]*, 24 October 1976.

Grechko, [Andrey Antonovich]. "Report by Marshal of the U.S.S.R." *Krasnaya Zvezda [Red Star]*, 28 March 1973.

Gribkov, A., Col. General. "Inculcating Demandingness." *Krasnaya Zvezda [Red Star]*, 4 June 1975.

Gudkov, V. "Transfer with Promotion." *Krasnaya Zvezda [Red Star]*, 14 October 1975.

Ishchenko, F., Lt. General. "Know How to Approach People." *Krasnaya Zvezda [Red Star]*, 10 September 1977.

Ivanov, N., Maj. General. "Socially Homogeneous Society." *Soviet Military Review*, October 1978.

Izgarshev, V., and Vikhreko, V. "On guard Over Peaceful Labor." *Krasnaya Zvezda [Red Star]*, 17 March 1977.

Jones, Christopher. "The Revolution in Military Affairs and Party Military Relations 1967-70." *Survey: A Journal of East-West Studies*, Winter 1974.

Kamalov, Yu. "Strictness and Concern." *Krasnaya Zvezda [Red Star]*, 12 December 1976.

Katz, Zev. "Sociology in the Soviet Union." *Problems of Communism*, May 1971.

Khobrostov, V. "V.I. Lenin, CPSU About Soldierly Discipline." *Military Historical Journal*, July 1977.

Klemchenko, L. "Until the Last Day of Service." *Krasnaya Zvezda [Red Star]*, 30 November 1976.

Kocherov, V. "Discipline—An Important Condition of Fulfilling Socialist Obligations." *Morskoi Sbornik [Navy Handbook]*, 7 (1977).

Kortun, V. "In Order That The Meeting Be Effective." *Krasnaya Zvezda [Red Star]*, 26 March 1977.

Kostikov, N. "Indoctrination of Cultural Behavior." *Krasnaya Zvezda [Red Star]*, 11 December 1976.

Krainin, L. "Strict Military Discipline—The Basis of High Combat Readiness of Troops, a Most Important Factor in the Achievement of Victory in Combat." *Kommunist Voorzhennykh Sil [Communist Defense Forces]*, 22 (1976).

Krivda, F. "With All the Fullness of Responsibility." *Krasnaya Zvezda [Red Star]*, 29 October 1976.

Kruzhin, Peter. "Soviet Military College." *Bulletin*, January 1971.

Kulakov, A. 'After a Promotion." *Krasnaya Zvezda [Red Star]*, 3 November 1976.

Lashchenko, P. "Formation of a Military Collective." *Voennii Vestnik [Military Herald]*, 9 (1976).

L'vov, V. "Reprimand." *Krasnaya Zvezda [Red Star]*, 17 October 1976.

Lyapkalo, B. "How They Taught the Lieutenant a Lesson." *Krasnaya Zvezda [Red Star]*, 29 January 1977.

Milovidov, A. "The Growth of the Role of the Morale Factor in War." *Military Historical Journal*, 3 (1977).

Mironenko. "The Fight Against Alcoholism in the U.S.S.R." *Bulletin*, September 1967.

Nikiforov, F., Col. "Behind the Palisade of Exactingness. "*Krasnaya Zvezda [Red Star]*, 11 June 1976.

Odom, William E. "The Militarization of Soviet Society." *Problems of Communism*, September-October 1976.

Ovchararov, I. "Teach Them to be Devoted, Determined, and Fearless." *Znamenosets [Standard-bearer]*, January 1978.

Pekarskii, B. "Help—Not Tutelage." *Krasnaya Zvezda [Red Star]*, 24 November 1976.

Pogrebtsov, O. "Is the Evaluation Objective?" *Krasnaya Zvezda [Red Star]*, 1 July 1976.

Prochenko. "Compulsory Treatment for Drunks, Addicts." *Sovetskaya Yustitsia [Soviet Justice]*, June 1974.

Provozin. V. "Culture and Discipline." *Krasnaya Zvezda [Red Star]*, November 1976.

Shakhuorostov, G. "And If Without Tutelage." *Krasnaya Zvezda [Red Star]*, 19 October 1976.

Shevkun, N. "In the Center of Attention—Competition." *Krasnaya Zvezda [Red Star]*, 29 January 1977.

Shelyag, V., Rear Admiral. "The Educational Force of the Military Collective.." "*Kommunist Vooruzhennykh Sil [Communist Defense Forces]*, April 1975.

Shenkar, I. "Awash in a Sea of Vodka: Drunkenness in Russia." *Horizon*, Winter 1976.

Shkadov, I., General. "Officer Efficiency Reports." *Krasnaya Zvezda [Red Star]*, 7 January 1978.

Shshnev, V., Major General. "The Rank of Officer Carries Obligations." *Kommunist Vooruzhennykh Sil [Communist Defense Forces]*, January 1978.

Skrylnik, A., Cpt. "Ideological Indoctrination: An Overall Approach." *Krasnaya Zvezda [Red Star]*, 3 August 1977.

Smith, D. "On Maneuvers With the Red Army." *Nation*, 20 May 1978.

Studentov, V. "The Officer Grows in the Collective." *Krasnaya Zvezda [Red Star]*, 13 October 1976.

Sukhorukov, D., COl. General. "Initiative, Self-Reliance." *Krasnaya Zvezda [Red Star]*, 28 March 1978.

Tabunov, N. "Soldiers and the Soldiers' Collective." *Kommunist Vooruzhennykh Sil [Communist Defense Forces]*, 24 December 1976.

Teplov, Yu. "The Bitter Taste of Criticism." *Krasnaya Zvezda [Red Star]*, 21 September 1977.

Tryshin, V. "Objectively and Honestly." *Krasnaya Zvezda [Red Star]*, 11 August 1976.

Vigor, P.H. "Soviet Armed Forces on Exercise." *Bullein*, October 1971.

Volkogonox, D., Maj. General. "The Comprehensive Approach in ideological Indoctrination of Soviet Fightingmen." *Voyenno-Istoricheskiy Zhurnal [Military Historical Journal]*, March 1978.

_____. "Moral Conflict," *Sovietskii Voin [Soviet Forces]*, 12 (1976).

Volkov, A., Maj. General. "The Power of Example." *Krasnaya Zvezda [Red Star]*, 25 October 1977.
_____. "Measure of Responsibility." *Krasnaya Zvezda [Red Star]*, 15 April 1976.
Yaroslavskii, M. "One for the Road for a Draftee." *Krasnaya Zvezda [Red Star]*, 15 October 1976.
Yerzunov, M. "An Important Factor in Enhancing Combat Readiness." *Krasnaya Zvezda [Red Star]*, 16 July 1976.
Zabavskaya, L. "The Whole World Studies Russian." *Soviet Military Review*, October 1978.
Zinoviev, B. "The Tact of a Commander." *Krasnaya Zvezda [Red Star]*, Octover 1976.

Magazines

"Be a Disciplined Soldier." *Kommunist Vooruzhennykh Sil [Communist Defense Forces]*, November 1975.
"Heighten Discipline and Organization." *Voennii Vestnik [Military Herald]*, June 1977.
"Insults." *Krasnaya Zvezda [Red Star]*, 29 March 1977.
"In the Interests of Discipline and Regulation Order." *Krasnaya Zvezda [Red Star]*, 11 January 1977.
"Know and Fulfill the Requirements of the Regulations." *Krasnaya Zvezda [Red Star]*, 10 February 1977.
"Know and Strictly Fulfill the Requirements of the Soldiers' Regulations." *Kommunist Vooruzhennykh Sil [Communist Defense Forces]*, vol. 21, 1975.
"Lack of Training Equipment." *Krasnaya Zvezda [Red Star]*, 10 December 1970, p. 2.
"Legal Indoctrination and Discipline." *Voennii Vestnik [Military Herald]*, June 1977.
"Life in the Soviet Army." *Time*, 4 May 1970, p. 46.
"Military Commissioning School—A Model of Regulation Order." *Krasnaya Zvezda [Red Star]*, 19 October 1976.
"Military Driver." *Krasnaya Zvezda [Red Star]*, 6 September 1977.
"75 Mutiny Cited in Soviet Journal." *Baltimore Sun*, 5 February 1977.
"On the Level of the Party's Requirements." *Krasnaya Zvezda [Red Star]*, July 1976.
"Organization of Military Instruction Cadres." *Krasnaya Zvezda [Red Star]*, 28 April 1971, p. 2.
"Persistent Evil." *Komolskaya Pravada [Communist Truth]*, 30 November 1967, pp. 6–7.
"Strengthening Legality and Discipline of Troops." *Krasnaya Zvezda [Red Star]*, 9 July 1971, p. 2.
"Strengthen the Authority of Sergeants and Petty Officers." *Krasnaya Zvezda [Red Star]*, 15 May 1976, p. 1.
"Teach What is Necessary in Battle." *Krasnaya Zvezda [Red Star]*, 24 January 1978, p. 1.
"The Company Political Worker." *Krasnaya Zvezda [Red Star]*, 8 July 1971, p. 1.
Time, 11 October 1976, p. 31 (Soviet Ground Crew Drinking in Siberia to Relieve Boredom.)
"Towards a New Rise in Ideological Work in the Forces." *Krasnaya Zvezda [Red Star]*, 1 November 1972.

Newspapers

"Battle Traditions Increase." *Izvestia*, 11 January 1967, p. 3.
Binder, David. "Soviet Defector Depicts Grim Life at MiG-25 Base." *The New York Times*, 13 January 1977.
"Everyday Life of a Paratrooper." *Pravada*, 30 January 1968, p. 6.
"Everyday Life of Soldiers." *Pravda*, 20 February 1967, p. 6.

Grechko. "Army of October." *Izvestia*, 23 February 1967, p. 6.

"Holiday for Tank Troops." *Pravda*, 11 September 1967, p. 2.

Izvestia, 26 October 1967, p. 1 (New Military Service System).

Izvestia, 23 February 1971, p. 4 (Profile of a Military Base in Siberia).

"Life in the Ground Forces (Rockets)." *Izvestia*, 8 January 1967, p. 5.

"Life of the Soviet Armed." *Izvestia*, 22 February 1967, p. 1.

"Man in a Fieldcoat." *Pravada*, 23 February 1967, p. 2.

"Our Army." *Pravda*, 23 February 1967, p. 1.

"People's Armor (Volunteer Societies for Cooperation with the Armed Forces)." *Izvestia*, 15 January 1967, p. 1.

Pravda, 3 July 1967, p. 3 (Soviet Military Academy Students).

Pravda, 8 July 1967, p. 6 (Soviet Army Training Camp).

"Report on Maneuvers."' *Pravda*, 25 September 1967, p. 6

"Report on Maneuvers." *Pravda*, 26 September 1967, p.2.

Pravda, 24 October 1967, p. 2 (Ideology in Armed Forces).

Pravda, 25 October 1967, p. 1 (New Compulsory Military Service System).

Pravda, 8 March 1969, p. 6 (Military Training & Sports).

Pravda, 22 February 1971, p. 4 (Life of an Individual Soldier).

"Soldier's Leisure Time." *Izvestia*, 24 February 1971, p. 4.

"Soldier's Tea." *Pravda*, 11 August 1977.

The New York Times, 17 October 1967, p. 1 (Defection of Lt. Col. Runge).

The New York Times, 22 October 1967, p. 7 (New Compulsory Mili-service Law).

The New York Times, 16 February 1968, p. 21 (Literary Gazette Calls for Rationing of Liquor).

The New York Times, 22 April 1968, p. 1 (CIA & W. Ger. report on a Soviet defection).

The New York Times, 24 October 1968, p. 1 (Soviet Naval Officers Arrested).

The New York Times, 25 January 1970, p. 3 (Secret Central Committee concerning strange penalties for drunkenness).

The New York Times, 29 March 1973, p. 7 (Gun battle between Soviet M.Ps and deserters in East Germany).

The New York Times, 3 December 1973, p. 9 (Soviet military extends tour of duty).

The New York Times, 7 September 1976, p. 1 (Belenko defects).

The New York Times, 10 September 1976, p. 24 (Belenko defection).

The New York Times, 7 January 1977, p. 5 (Belenko story that Soviet pilots ordered to commit suicide rather than surrender or risk missing a target. Reported in West German Magazine *Stern*, 6 January).

Miscellaneous

Kruzhin, Peter. "The Principal Features of the Latest All Service Military Regulations." Radio Liberty Research Reports, November 4, 1976.

Mentality of the Soviet Soldier. Ottawa: Director-General of Intelligence, 1974.

Physical Training of the Soviet Soldier. DDB-2680-48-78, April 1978.

Paporshchick—A New Rank in the Soviet Army. Garmish-Partenkirchen, West Germany: Army Institute for Advanced Russian Studies, 1974.

Segal, Boris M. "The Incidence of Suicides in the Soviet Union." *Radio Liberty Dispatch*, February 2, 1977.

Soviet Military Schools. DDB-2680-52-78, June 1978.

Soviet Ground Forces Training Program. DDB-1100-200-78, July 1978.

Review of Soviet Ground Forces. RSGF1-77, August 1977.

About the Author

RICHARD A. GABRIEL is Professor of Politics at St. Anselm's College in Manchester, New Hampshire. A Major in the U.S. Army Reserve, Dr. Gabriel is assigned to the Soviet Division of the Directorate of Foreign Intelligence in Washington. His earlier books include *Crisis in Command, Managers and Gladiators: Direction of Change in the Army* (Paul L. Savage) and *Program Evaluation: A Social Science Approach.*